PARENT/TEACHR

'98

...ATIONAL PROGRAMMING

A How-To-Do-It Manual For Librarians

RHEA JOYCE RUBIN

*HOW-TO-DO-IT MANUALS
FOR LIBRARIES*

Number 36

NEAL-SCHUMAN PUBLISHERS, INC.
New York, London

Published by Neal-Schuman Publishers, Inc.
100 Varick Street
New York, NY 10013

Copyright © 1993 by Rhea Joyce Rubin

Printed and bound in the United States of America

Library of Congress Cataloging-in-Publication Data

Rubin, Rhea Joyce.
    Intergenerational programming : a how-to-do-it manual for
librarians / Rhea Joyce Rubin.
        p. cm. — (How-to-do-it manuals for libraries ; no. 36)
    Includes bibliographical references and index.
    ISBN 1-55570-157-4
    1. Public libraries — United States. 2. Public libraries — United
States — Service to the aged. 3. Libraries, Children's — United
States. 4. Intergenerational relations — United States. I. Title.
II. Series.
Z711.7.R83   1993
027.6'22'0973—dc20   93-28617
                                                        CIP

CONTENTS

PREFACE

Intergenerational Programming: A How-To-Do-It Manual for Librarians has four main parts. The first describes the what and why of intergenerational programming and discusses the myriad benefits it holds for participants, library, and community. Part two presents planning and evaluation suggestions. The third part details successful library-based intergenerational programs. And part four gives some ideas of how to start "intergenerating" quickly and easily.

Intended as a practical guide, this volume features:

- Lots of real-life program examples, including sample flyers and forms and words of advice from practitioners.
- Many references to print and nonprint resources in each section and six resource lists in the appendix.
- Easy-to-use planning, budgeting, and action plan forms in Part 2 and Part 3.

Much of this book is based on a simple survey sent to libraries identified through the literature or through word-of-mouth. Ninety-five programs were queried; sixty-one responded or were reached by telephone. If your library has an intergenerational program, *please* share it! A survey form for your use follows.

INTERGENERATIONAL LIBRARY PROGRAMS SURVEY

Name of Program:_____

Person Submitting Form:_____

Address:_____

Telephone:_____

Date:_____

1. Year program began:

2. Brief description of program:

3. Target age groups:

4. Is program still ongoing? If not, when and why was it discontinued?

5. Is the program offered in conjunction with any other agency or organization? If so, who?

6. What adjectives best describe the participants' response to the program?

7. What words of advice do you have for other librarians interested in trying intergenerational programming?

8. Additional comments:

Please send the completed form to Intergenerational Survey, Rubin Consulting, 5860 Heron Drive, Oakland, CA 94618-2628. Thanks!

ACKNOWLEDGMENTS

Many people have contributed to *Intergenerational Programming* by sharing their own experiences with intergenerational programming or by referring me to yet another program. I thank especially the librarians in Texas, Ohio, Illinois, and California with whom I have worked on intergenerational programs, and consultants: Barbara Crosby and Vicky Crossan of Texas; Millie Fry and Sue McCleaf Nespeca of northern Ohio; Kathleen Weibel and Miriam Pollock of northern Illinois; and Bessie Egan of California.

I am grateful, too, to Jane Angelis, of the Illinois Intergenerational Initiative, who shared the results of her survey of intergenerational programs. And to Mary Jo Brazil, of the Vintage Health Library, for her emergency reference service.

Lynne Martin Erickson and Kathryn Leide, of Bi-Folkal Productions, Inc.—who have designed my own intergenerational brochure and bibliographies, and with whom I have done training over these past ten years—deserve kudos for opening their files and rolodexes to me.

Lars, computer assistant exemplar, merits praise for upgrading my monitor, printer, and software—all during this book's preparation.

Thanks to the Berman clipping service for its invaluable contributions.

And special thanks to my beautiful daughter, Hannah, and my wonderful husband, Larry, who were patient (almost always) and encouraging (always) during the year of writing this book.

PART I
DEFINITIONS AND DEMOGRAPHICS

¶ WHAT AND WHY

INTERGENERATIONAL PROGRAMMING IS...

Activities or programs that increase cooperation, interaction, or exchange between any two generations. It involves the sharing of skills, knowledge, or experience between young and old.

Open any newspaper and you can read about the new generation gap—tensions between older adults and children's advocates for their piece of a shrinking social services pie. Turn on the television and you can see yet another program about the desperate need for children's daycare—and for senior daytime assistance. Glance at a magazine and you can read about the fear of aging by children—and the fear of teens by older adults. Read a professional journal for the latest news on shrinking library budgets. Everywhere, it seems, we are confronted with either/or decisions on library services, economic priorities, and social issues. Yet combining services for people at both ends of the age spectrum (and in between) is too rarely mentioned.

Instead of choosing between serving the old and the young, we can do both. Numerous towns are doing this in the daycare arena by combining elder daycare with children's daycare or by establishing senior daycare in schools or starting before-and-after school programs in nursing homes. In libraries, too, the intergenerational approach is beginning to take root.

Intergenerational programs combine people of more than one age group in a mutually beneficial, mutually enjoyable activity. One purpose is to share commonalties and celebrate differences across the age span, increasing understanding and enjoyment. Another is to desegregate library services and to promote interdependence, rather than separatism, among our users. A third is to make the most effective use of our limited resources.

The National Council on the Aging, Inc. defines intergenerational projects as "activities or programs that increase cooperation, interaction, or exchange between any two generations. It involves the sharing of skills, knowledge, or experience between young and old." Note that this definition stresses *reciprocity*. In other words, travel film programs which may attract people of various ages and circulation departments which serve everyone are *not* intergenerational programs; they have not been designed for mutual exchange. The definition also mentions *any two generations*, which is significant as many people think of intergenerational programs as only involving the very young and the very old. In this book we will highlight programs involving preschoolers, school-age children and teenagers as well as middle-aged, older, and very old adults.

Although intergenerational services are new, relationships across the lifespan are not. As recently as a few decades ago, most Americans lived in multigeneration families and participated in community events and entertainment for all ages. As Jane Angelis, Director of the Illinois Intergenerational Initiative, reminds us: "The innovation is not the interaction between old and young;

3

rather, the innovation is how they gain access to one another: the linking of generations" (Angelis, "Genesis. . ." 1992).

WHO ARE THE OLDER ADULTS?

Who are the older adults in 1990s America? The 50-year-old person pushing both a wheelchair and a stroller? The frail, bedridden nursing home patient? The newly retired golf players who take lengthy, expensive vacations? The president of the bank, who is also president of the library board?

One in every eight Americans is 65 or over. These 31.1 million people (according to the 1990 census) make older adults the largest minority population in America. We now have more older adults than the total population of the Scandinavian countries combined. This group is growing more rapidly than any other segment of our population, as well. The number of older Americans increased by 21% from 1980-1990 as compared to an increase of 8% for the under-65 population. By 2020, one in every five Americans (20%) will be 65 or over. Because the human life span (that is, the potential life span based on laboratory experiments) is 120, and the age of first serious infirmity is increasing, the average American is living longer each year.

Of older adults, the over 85 age group is growing the fastest. The average life span has been steadily increasing since the 1950s and is now approximately 80 overall. About 1.2% of the population (or 3 million people) are over 85 now. That number is six times what it was 90 years ago and is expected by conservative demographers to grow to seven times (or 20 million) in the next 90 years. (Other researchers expect dramatic leaps to 72 million in the over 85 age group).

According to the 1990 census, only one of every ten older people is nonwhite although ethnic diversity among older adults is increasing. Demographers expect minority populations to represent 23 percent of the elderly population by 2020 and 35 percent by 2050. The Hispanic elderly will show the greatest increase—from approximately 4 percent to 15 percent. These projections assume continuation of present birth, death, and immigration (legal and illegal) patterns.

The disproportionately low number of older people of color today is due to the extreme differences in life expectancy by race.

Although the average American of any race and gender lives to 81.9 years, the averages vary by race from 59 to 86. The average white woman lives to 84 and the average white man to 80, while the average Asian woman lives to 86 and the average Asian man to 79. The average African-American woman lives to 75 and the average African-American man to 68 while the average Native American woman lives to 72 and the average Native American man to 59. Note that African-Americans account for 8 percent of the 65 and over age group in the 1990 census; the other races combined account for only 3 percent of the older population. It is difficult to obtain figures for hispanic elders because they may be of any race, but the current estimate of life expectancy by the National Hispanic Council on the Aging is 55 for both men and women.

Older adults live in every area of the United States, although half of them live in only nine states: California (three million), New York, Florida (2.4 million each), Pennsylvania, Texas, Illinois, Ohio, Michigan, and New Jersey (over one million each). Eight states have 15 percent or more of their population over 65 (the U.S. average is 12.6 percent). One-third of older people live in rural areas although most services for them are in urban centers.

Let's put these demographics of older adulthood into an intergenerational perspective. In 1900, 4 percent of the US population was 65 or over while 44 percent was younger than 19 years. In 2000, there will be no such gap. Approximately 14 percent of the US population will be 65 or over—and about the same will be younger than 19. One more thing older adults and youth will have in common!

It is essential to recognize the broad range of people encompassed in the term "older adult." Current nomenclature defines "middle age" as 50-plus, "middle old" as 66-74, "old" as 75-84, and "very old" as over 85. Besides age differences, older adulthood encompasses a full array of health and impairment. For example, despite contemporary mythology, less than 5 percent of people 65 and older reside in nursing homes/long-term healthcare facilities. Although 25 to 50 percent of older adults will be in such a facility at some time during their lives, on any day the institutionalized elderly are a small portion of the older population. Another myth is that all older people are wealthy. Although the average income level of older people is higher than it has ever been, 25 percent of people 65 and over live at or below the poverty level.

Increasingly, older adults are retirees. Although women are working longer than they used to, men are retiring earlier and earlier. Over 75 percent of people now retire under 65 years of age.

- Only 5% of today's youth see their grandparents on a regular basis.

- 70% of grandparents live at least two hours from their grandchildren.

- For the first time, there are more Americans 65 and over than there are teenagers.

- By 2050 we will have more people 65 and over than youth 19 and younger.

- The fastest growing segment of the US population is people 85 and over.

These means they have an average of 16.9 years of retirement—a longer period than the average number of years spent in school!

WHO ARE THE YOUTH?

Of course, the youth of America are a diverse group too. Though most people are surprised to learn of the variety within older adulthood, we are accustomed to thinking of childhood and young adulthood as having numerous distinct separations.

As of 1990, preschool children comprise 7.3 percent of the U.S. population. School-age children (ages six through 17) are 18.9 percent of our population. Young adults (ages 18 through 24) represent 12 percent.

The proportion of youth to adults in this country is shrinking. For example, in 1900, 44 percent of Americans were younger than nineteen. By 1980, this had dropped to 28 percent. In 2000 the number will be close to 14 percent. Although the actual number of youth will increase until 2000, the percentage is decreasing. After 2000, the total number of children will begin decreasing as well. As the Children's Defense Fund states "Children and young adults are becoming scarce resources" (*State of America's Children* 1991).

Currently, 29.7 percent of children under 18 are members of minority groups. This is up from 28 percent in 1985 and is expected to reach 32.7 percent by 2000 and 45 percent by 2080.

Children are the largest group of poor people in America today. According to the 1990 Census, nearly 18 percent of children under 18 (and more than 20 percent of children under five) live in poverty. Families with children under age five are almost twice as likely to be poor as families without; 10 percent of American families live in poverty but 18.3 percent of families with young children live in poverty. And 57.3 percent of female-headed households with small children live below the poverty line.

Of today's children, only 29 percent live in the traditional nuclear family. Instead of the classic American household of two married adults with two or more of their own children, kids are living in blended families with step-siblings and step-parents or in single parent households (usually female-headed). Twenty-five percent of all American adolescents (and 45 percent of teens in inner-city neighborhoods) are growing up in one-parent families. More and more often children are being raised by grandparents;

although this has not been uncommon in black and hispanic families, it is a relatively new phenomenon in the white culture.

Another new aspect of family life in 1990s America is "latchkey children." These are children (approximately five to 12 million or 20-25 percent of all school age children according to the National PTA in 1987) who are unsupervised after school until evening when a parent or grandparent returns from work. This phenomenon is especially relevant to libraries. A survey conducted in 1984 by the Los Angeles County Public Library System revealed that in 50 of their 92 facilities, a total of more than 1,000 children were using the library for daycare purposes after school.One national study (Dowd, 1988) found that in three-fourths of responding public libraries, an average number of 21 children aged 10 to 12 years of age were unattended in the library three to five days per week from 3 p.m. to 6 p.m.

WHAT DO OLDER ADULTS AND YOUTH HAVE IN COMMON?

Researchers and policymakers note that young people and older adults have many similarities in our society. They are both marginalized and often invisible. They are more likely than other age groups to be poor. They are usually unemployed and therefore not considered contributors to society. In many cases they are powerless and dependent on middle-aged adults in some facet of their lives. Psychologists and program planners comment that both children and old people tend to have less rigid expectations and to be more frank in their communication. They may also share an unconventional sense of time and place less emphasis on present-tense objectives.

2 BENEFITS OF INTERGENERATIONAL PROGRAMMING

Intergenerational programming in libraries offers a myriad of benefits for everyone involved: the youth, the older adults, the library, and the greater community.

FOR YOUTH

For children and teens, intergenerational projects provide an opportunity for a personal relationship with an elder. Only 5 percent of youth today can see their grandparent(s) on a regular basis, and few have regular contact with any other older person. A 1986 Roper poll showed that only 63 percent of families with children seven to 17 years old eat dinner together frequently. A recent national survey found that almost 20 percent of the sixth through 12th graders polled reported that they had not had a ten-minute conversation with a parent or grandparent within the last month.

This missed opportunity is important for children and teens because they are naturally curious—about old age as well as other topics elders can discuss. Educators and psychologists stress that youth need to see the entire life cycle to understand their own place in the now and to envision their own futures. It is essential that youth meet positive role models of aging in order to develop positive attitudes toward it, attitudes that will help them in their own aging process and enlighten their approach to social issues concerning older adults.

Also, sociologists link the growth in gang and other delinquent behavior among teens to their need for strong family or intergenerational relationships and to their need for extracurricular activities. According to the U.S. Department of Education, 30 percent of all teens (and up to 40 percent in ethnic, urban, or poor families) participate in no extracurricular activities such as scouting, youth clubs, religious youth groups, summer programs, or non-school sports. Library intergenerational programs can address both the need for intergenerational contact and the need for extracurricular activities.

There are many other reasons that young people—especially teenagers—need to have personal relationships with older adults.

"Life is a country that the old have seen and lived in. Those who have to travel through it can only learn from them."

—Joseph Joubert

One is to receive the unconditional acceptance that they do not receive from teachers, parents, and other authorities. Older adults also offer youth the long view, a perspective that is novel to them. Elders can serve as mentors for teens who too often only have media models to follow.

For young children, intergenerational programs assist in the development of prosocial behaviors, such as sharing, helping, and cooperating. For all young people, interactions with older adults promote empathy and an understanding of physical limitations which often accompany aging.

Finally, older adults have life experiences that only they can share, and that young people can learn no other way. Whether these experiences and wisdom are shared through living history, oral history, storytelling, or other modes, older adults are a unique resource for young people. Similarly, elders have skills which must be shared for young people to learn them.

"When an old person dies, a library burns"

—African saying

FOR OLDER ADULTS

Seventy percent of older adults live at least two hours from their grandchildren. And most older adults have little contact with other youth due to segregation caused by mobility, housing, and other problems. Many older people express a need to interact with younger people, to understand and enjoy them. The enthusiasm, energy, and innocence of children is joyous to older adults who remember themselves that way.

One of the developmental needs of older adulthood is to reminisce, to re-experience earlier (and often healthier) times in their lives. Interaction with youth can assist adults in this life review process.

According to gerontologists and psychologists, older adults also need to feel that they will live on beyond their own physical life and that they have helped guide the next generation. Intergenerational programming encourages older people to share their skills, experiences, and perspectives, in part to ensure that these will live on.

"Add life to the years that have been added to life." International Federation on Aging/ UN International Day for the Elderly

For isolated elders, a personal relationship with a younger person can reduce loneliness and social isolation and thereby improve self-esteem. For other older adults, intergenerational activities are a positive, fulfilling use of retirement time as well as a source of fun.

FOR THE LIBRARY

Intergenerational programs break down long entrenched barriers between age-distinct departments. In all too many libraries, children's services and adult services are kept totally separate. One children's librarian involved with an intergenerational program reported in the survey the author sent, "It was most gratifying to work with the adult staff for the first time; I felt it was one of the best things to come out of the program." Intergenerational programs require library staff to share ideas and resources across departmental lines and to cooperate.

In times of shrinking library budgets, such cooperation also stretches tight resources. Rather than two or more departments developing separate special Valentine's Day events, for example, one intergenerational event can be planned. The craft skills of the children's department can be combined with the outreach expertise of the adult services department. In addition to spreading people and material resources, such cooperation produces a new sense of *esprit de corps* in the library and stimulates a new sense of purpose among staff.

As one librarian reported in the author's survey: The concept of intergenerational programming is positive and constructive, and is an appropriate avenue for the public library to use in fulfilling its mission to serve the total community.

The ability to serve a greater spectrum of the community through intergenerational programs positions the library well in the city or county. The library may be on the cutting edge of intergenerational services which will soon be touted by the parks department, the housing office, and the nutrition programs. Such

"In a fast-changing society like ours, the young ones are the pathfinders and pioneers. They are the experts on today and tomorrow, the people who feel most at home in the now."

—Margaret Mead

innovation usually yields media and political attention to the library. Also new partnerships with other agencies in the community (for example schools, nursing homes, social service providers) often result from intergenerational programs; additional colleagues and supporters in the community can then have many other unexpected benefits.

A final benefit of intergenerational programming is that it may lead to a new source of volunteers (see chapter six) and it produces new library users, young and old.

FOR THE GREATER COMMUNITY

Most communities are aware of the growing and diverse needs of the different population groups, including all the age categories, represented in their area. Intergenerational programming allows a community to respond to these needs through an existing agency, the library.

Because of the interagency approach of most intergenerational programs (again, see chapter four), they lead to increased communication among segments of the community and new partnerships among agencies and individuals. The resources, skills, and experience in the community—from the library and from the individual elders involved—are utilized more effectively.

Improved communication and new partnerships then lead to a more cohesive community spirit. Meanwhile, local historical and cultural traditions (whether through a town history project or an annual holiday ritual) are maintained and celebrated.

PART II
PLANNING AND EVALUATION

A recent study of six intergenerational programs found "four common components present in the creation of an intergenerational program: a need, crisis or problem; a committed responsive leader; a source of encouragement and support; and an accessible system for linking young and old. Each of the programs involved a creative process that generated an idea and a system bringing young and old together. . ." (Angelis 1992). In this section, we will discuss the creation of a program from planning through evaluation.

3 THE GOLDEN RULES

For planning intergenerational programs, as for everything else in life, there are a few golden rules to keep in mind.

Stress interactive programs: Intergenerational programs must be *actively* intergenerational. In other words, the intergenerational component must not be accidental. For example, your library circulation desk serves people of all ages but it is not an intergenerational program. Similarly, a travel lecture may attract an audience spanning several generations but it is not an intergenerational program either—unless interaction across the generations is a significant part (and objective). This idea becomes fuzzy with another example: retired volunteers deliver library books to a preschool daycare center. Although the program goal is to provide a service to youngsters while employing seniors, it would not be an exemplary intergenerational program either because interaction is not encouraged. If those same senior volunteers read to the children, and talk to them, the integenerational goal is met.

Involve young and old in the planning: Older adults are used to controlling their own lives and making their own decisions; they do not appreciate activities based on well-meaning assumptions, planned for them without their input. Children and teens are accustomed to being told what to do, but enjoy the opportunity to represent themselves. By including both young and old in the planning process you accomplish a number of objectives: you model the intergenerational approach your program will take, you ensure that the activities planned are feasible and appropriate, and you create a sense of ownership of the program that will help you when you work on publicity, fundraising, and volunteer recruitment.

Educate youth and older adults about each other: Unfortunately, most of us have fears and misconceptions about people unlike ourselves, including people of different ages. For example, young children assume all older people are near death. Young adults often assume that seniors cannot understand the passions of youth. Older adults fear that teens are wild. All of these stereotypes derive from media images, segregation by age in housing and social activities, and a lack of everyday contact with people of different ages. Intergenerational programs are an opportunity to educate participants about the entire life span. Indeed, many elementary and high school curricula now include "Learning About Aging" to introduce children to the whole life cycle.

Do not patronize either age group: Staff members also have preconceived notions about age groups. It is important that your program avoid such stereotypes. For example, staff will often assume that people over a certain age cannot see well. Although a decrease in visual acuity is a common facet of aging, new modes of eye surgery and advances in eyeglasses mean that many older adults see as well as young people. All participants in your program, young and old, must be treated foremost as individuals. They are the best judges of abilities, needs, and interests.

Guarantee mutual benefits: Some intergenerational programs focus on only one of the participating age groups. For example, helping-hand projects in which teens assist older adults with household chores. Unless a benefit for the young volunteer is built into the program, volunteer turnover will be high. In a good intergenerational program, all participants both give and receive.

Maximize the benefits by allowing for active reflection on the intergenerational experience: Because few older adults have regular contact with youngsters and vice versa, an intergenerational program must have an educational component, as discussed above. A related need is the opportunity for all participants to reflect on and discuss the new experience. For the program planner, such "debriefing" can serve as a form of evaluation as well because the participants' reactions and comments can be used to perfect the next program.

Encourage one-to-one relationships: This golden rule seems especially difficult for librarians who are accustomed to group programming and concerned with protecting individuals' privacy in library matters. But one-to-one relationships are not uncommon in the library. For example, a patron may have a special relationship with one reference librarian who always answers her questions. A librarian may have a favorite patron he looks forward to seeing. The volunteers who visit homebound patrons see them one at a time, in their own homes. In intergenerational programs, too, one-to-one friendships are encouraged whenever possible.

Use multiculturally diverse activities: Given America's changing demographics, and the current dialogue on multiculturalism, this golden rule should go without saying. Any intergenerational activity, whether storytelling, holiday celebration, or theatrics, is an opportunity for multiculturally diverse materials and approaches.

Start small (but think large): Starting small is a golden rule for any new project or service because a seed project allows for maximum creativity and minimum risk. It is easier to sell a reluctant administrator or colleague on a small, discrete project with well-defined expectations. And it is easier to succeed with a first attempt which has controlled objectives and outcomes. After impressing everyone (including yourself?) and learning from the inevitable problems, a larger ongoing intergenerational program is almost guaranteed.

Cooperate with another agency: Interagency cooperation is such a vital principle that the entire next chapter is devoted to it.

4 INTERAGENCY COOPERATION

According to *Generations Together*, an intergenerational project and clearinghouse in Pittsburgh, successful intergenerational programs universally share certain characteristics. One of these is collaboration among agencies.

Working with at least one other organization or institution has many advantages. Some of these are:

- Each agency contributes its expertise. For example, the local Area Agency on Aging can provide the knowledge of your community's elders while the library provides its special expertise.
- Project personnel time is split between the agencies. In other words, each organization provides partial staff support and ends up with a total program.
- Operating costs are shared by the participating agencies. Some materials, for example books owned by the library or a van owned by the daycare center, can be donated to further reduce cash outlay.
- When obstacles loom large, enthusiasm and encouragement are forthcoming from the partner agency.
- Some anticipated problems are avoided altogether. For example, if finding interested teens is a concern, collaboration with a youth organization may ensure teen attendance. If meeting space is tight in the library, partnership with the senior center which has a multi-purpose room may be the answer.

Keep in mind that the library is a highly respected community institution with a lot to offer. We may take ourselves for granted, but other agencies and organizations don't! Some of the library's appeals as an interagency partner are its neutrality, credibility, and visibility. The fact is that the library disseminates local materials and information, has a community bulletin board and meeting space, and has a technical expertise that few other agencies can claim.

POSSIBLE INTERGENERATIONAL PARTNERS

To locate groups of youth, start your search by contacting:

- Schools
- Headstart programs
- PTA
- Teen clubs
- Scout and campfire troops (who must participate in community activities to earn badges)
- 4-H and similar programs
- School (or junior) service clubs
- Daycare centers
- Group residential homes
- Churches and synagogues
- Parks and recreation departments
- Other social service and educational agencies.

To find older adults, try contacting one of these groups in your area:

- Area Agency on Aging (AAA)
- American Association of Retired Persons (AARP) chapter
- National Association of Retired Federal Employees (NARFE)
- Retired Senior Volunteer Program (RSVP)—a program of ACTION
- Retired Teachers Association (RTA) chapter—a unit of AARP
- Service Corps of Retired Executives (SCORE)—a program of the Small Business Administration
- Senior Centers
- Council of Senior Citizens
- Senior Community Service Employment Program
- Foster Grandparent Program—a program of ACTION
- Adult day care centers
- Nursing homes
- Lifecare communities
- Colleges
- Elderhostel programs
- Alumni groups
- Gray Panthers chapter
- Service organizations
- Senior residences
- Senior nutrition sites
- Churches and synagogues
- Community centers
- Other social service and educational agencies

Note that the national addresses for many of these organizations are listed in the Resources section at the end of this book.

Once you find one or more partners for your intergenerational initiative, be sure to build a special relationship with them. Audrey Ryan, the director of "Connections" of the Miami-Dade County Library in Florida states that you must develop a good understanding of what their agencies do, what resources they have, and what services they may need. Get yourself on their mailing lists and read their publications. Become actively involved with their services by writing pieces for their newsletters or by serving on one of their committees. Cultivate contacts with their agency staff by meeting for informal lunches, providing SDI (selective dissemination of information) service to them, and by keeping them informed of all the library's plans all year long—and not just when you need them.

PREPARATION

According to Sallie Johnson of the Elverita Lewis Foundation, there are five C's to keep in mind when starting an intergenerational program. These are: concept, community, coordination, constituents, and cooperation (Johnson 1985).

Concept: This is the original intergenerational activity idea, shaped by needs assessment and a program design created by an advisory committee.

Community: Refers to the need for interagency cooperation and community involvement.

Coordination: The daily work of the project coordinator(s), including budgeting, calendar, staff and volunteer recruitment and training, and reporting.

Constituents: The program participants, recruited through interagency involvement, publicity, or both. The constituents are the purpose and the reward for all library programming.

Cooperation: Refers to the need for communication, recognition, evaluation, and outreach to ensure that your program continues successfully.

GENERATING IDEAS

"If you fail to plan, you plan to fail."

If you already have an idea for an intergenerational program, start by finding another agency or organization to work with. Next, build a planning committee.

If you don't yet have an idea, you may want to make contacts with other agencies and even convene a planning committee first— then everyone can help to generate ideas. Or you may wish to have a number of idea alternatives to present to the committee first. In that case, start by studying the program models described in Part III and see which appeal to you and appear suitable for your community.

Or, ask yourself what programs the library now offers which could be done intergenerationally. Could an intergenerational approach enhance them? What programs does another community agency offer which could be done intergenerationally with assistance from the library? Would an intergenerational approach strengthen them?

Another approach to generating program ideas is offered by Ronald Manheimer of the Center for Creative Retirement. He suggests making a grid. Across the top, list possible themes for the program. For example, history, stories, families, holidays. Down the left-hand side, list activities. For example, remembering, exploring, discussing, recording, dramatizing, writing. Think of a program for each intersection of the grid. For example, what about dramatizing history? Recording families? Writing about holidays? Discussing stories? You get the idea.

INTERGENERATIONAL PROGRAMMING CALENDAR

An easy way to generate program ideas, especially for short-term events, is to use holidays and commemorative weeks. Here are some you may wish to use:

January
New Year (America, Japan, Korea, Taiwan, Thailand)
Martin Luther King, Jr. Day (third Monday)
Eye and Health Care Month
National Hobby Month

February
Black History Month
Race Relations Day (14th)
New Year (China)
Tet (Vietnamese New Year)
Valentine's Day (14th)
Presidents' Day (third Monday)
American Heart Month
International Friendship Week (week beginning third Sunday)

March
National Women's History Month
National Teenagers' Day (21st)
National Employ the Older Worker Week (third week)
National Nutrition Month
Ramadan (Islamic)
Passover (Jewish)
Easter (Christian)

Save Your Vision Week (second week)
International Women's Day (8th)
Art Week (last full week)
Youth Day (China, 29th)

April
National Library Week (third week)
National Volunteer Week (third week)
Week of the Young Child (second week)
Festival of Ancestors (Chinese)
Earth Day (22nd)
World Health Day (7th)
Cancer Control Month
National Consumers' Week (third week)

May
Older Americans Month
Senior Center Week (second week)
Mother's Day (second Sunday)
National Nursing Home Week (second week)
National Hospital Week (Second week)
Cinco de Mayo (Mexican, 5th)
Children's Day (Japanese and Korean, 5th)
Jewish Heritage Month
Asian/Pacific American Heritage Month
Memorial Day (31st)
National Pet Week (first full week)
Better Speech and Hearing Month
Arthritis Month
• National Intergenerational Week (week beginning third Sunday)

June
Father's Day (third Sunday)
National Children's Day (13th)
Read America Week (second week)
National Adopt-A-Cat Month
Lesbian and Gay Pride Month
Juneteenth (African American, 19th)

July
Muharram (Islamic New Year)
Ratha-yatra (Hindu New Year)
Independence Day (U.S.)

Music for Life Week (first week)

August
Youth Day (Zambia, 6th)
National Smile Week (week beginning first Monday)

September
Grandparents' Day (first Sunday after Labor Day)
National Adult Day Care Week (third week)
National Hispanic Heritage Month
American Indian Day (fourth Friday)
Rosh Hashanah (Jewish New Year)
Banned Books Week (week beginning fourth Saturday)
National Library Card Sign-Up Month
International Literacy Day (8th)
National Dog Week (last week)

October
United Nations' Day for the Elderly (1st)
Universal Children's Week (first seven days)
Children's Day (first Monday)
National Adopt-A-Dog Month
Halloween (31st)

November
Thanksgiving (fourth Thursday)
National Young Readers' Day (19th)
National Children's Book Week (third week)
Children's Day (India, 14th)
National Make A Difference Day (14th)
National Alzheimer's Disease Awareness Month
National Caregivers' Week (week beginning with fourth Sunday)
American Education Week (first full week preceding Thanksgiving)
National Hospice Month
Veterans' Day (11th)
National Cat Week (first week)

December
Christmas (Christian, 25th)
Chanukah (Jewish)
Kwanzaa (African American week beginning 26th)
Universal Human Rights Month

INITIAL INTERAGENCY MEETING

Once you have some ideas in mind, set up a meeting with one or more other agencies to discuss them. Be sure to consider the following questions:

1. Are the ideas appropriate? Interesting? Capable of success?
2. How can the proposed program be mutually beneficial to both generations?
3. Is the idea applicable to both (all) agencies?
4. What assistance is already in place from each agency?
5. Which other community agencies can be partners in this? What assistance might they add? In planning? In operations?
6. Whose cooperation (inside each agency and outside) is needed?
7. Whose approval is needed?
8. What obstacles must be overcome to gain the support of administrators and colleagues?
9. Composition of advisory committee?

PLANNING COMMITTEE MEETING

After the advisory committee is in place, call a meeting to discuss these basic planning questions and to divide responsibility for answering them.

1. Are the ideas put forward appropriate? Interesting? Beneficial to both young and old? Capable of success?
2. If not, how can the ideas be adapted? Replaced?
3. Should any other agency/organization/constituent group be represented on the planning committee?
4. Can this project be done with existing staff?
5. How might volunteers be used? Recruited?
6. Will funding be needed? How much? Possible sources?
7. What materials and supplies will be needed? Possible source?
8. How will you publicize the program to get participants?
9. Where will the intergenerational activity take place? Is this the best location considering participants' transportation and scheduling concerns?
10. When will the activity place? How often? Duration?
11. What is the life span of the program? Is there a pilot phase?
12. How will success be measured?
13. How to ensure that it will last beyond the pilot phase?

"Remember the five C's:"
- Concept
- Community
- Coordination
- Constituents
- Cooperation

Once these questions are answered fully, the first phase of program planning is done!

SCHEDULING THE PROGRAM(S)

Scheduling programs for participants of varied ages can be difficult. The day and time best suited to one group may not be appropriate for another. For example, weekday mornings may be best for preschoolers but impossible for teens. Weekday evenings may be perfect for elementary school children but difficult for older adults. Similarly, location may be problematic depending on your community's transportation options.

These are the programming specifics which should be taken into account when you make scheduling decisions:

Optimal size of group: Is your program designed for a small group? For one-to-one activity? Keep in mind that some people (for example, those with difficulty hearing and young children) require very small groups.

Attention span: Small children and frail elders suffering from memory disorders usually have short attention spans. This may also be a problem for people on certain medications.

Need for quiet or privacy in program area: Will other programs be taking place in the same room? If so, what about noise level? For example, teens recording elders' oral histories will need quiet and privacy for sustained periods.

Space needs for program: How much space do you need? Can another activity share the space? Is there enough space for people using wheelchairs?

Transportation availability: Will participants be expected to get to the library, for example, by themselves? If so, is there convenient and safe parking? If not, who will provide transportation? Many older adults are concerned about public transportation or even a shared car if it does not bring them directly to their door. Many teens do not have cars and cannot or do not want to depend on their parents. Although transportation is most often mentioned by librarians as a potential obstacle to intergenerational programs, many older adult services have their own vans and many juvenile daycare services and some schools have contractual arrangements for transportation with local services or the city's mass transit system. This may be one facet of planning best left to another agency partner.

Accessibility for people with disabilities: Any program involving older adults must consider the probability of physical disabilities and prepare the setting with accessibility in mind.

Lighting and seating needs: Programs for children often assume that the kids sit on the floor and that lighting is not a major issue. Programs for older people, however, must provide for stable seating and adequate lighting.

Conflicting activities in community schedule: A common pitfall of program planners is to fail to consider the community's calendar. When are the high school's homecoming games? Not only high school students attend them. What about the local symphony concerts and bingo games? Be sure to choose a date and time with as few conflicts as possible for potential participants.

Daily schedule of participants: We've all heard of the program that flopped because the volunteers showed up—when the children were at recess, or the preschoolers were napping, or the nursing home residents were receiving medications. Know the daily schedule of your potential participants and choose a time accordingly.

Weather as an attendance factor: Is inclement weather a major factor in your community? It may be especially significant if participants are depending on public transportation, or if the program site is far off the beaten track.

SELECTION AND PREPARATION OF PARTICIPANTS AND STAFF

Now comes the selection and education of staff and volunteers, and the selection and preparation of the participants. The preparation varies depending on the ages of the participants, and how they are being contacted.

The easiest way to select participants and staff is to cooperate with an organization or agency that already has these in place. For example, if you want to find elementary school children, make the school or the after-school childcare center a project partner.

Similarly, if you need active, healthy older adults, team up with the senior center or a senior organization.

For some programs, the library may prefer to use its own existing groups. For example, you might connect the nursing home you are already serving with the members of the children's summer reading program you already sponsor.

Or you may decide to recruit participants one by one, as you do with most programs. In that case, publicity (discussed in chapter 7) is essential both to recruit participants and volunteers, as needed.

Once your participants, staff, and volunteers are known, they need preparation for the intergenerational program. Usually, they are familiar with only one age range and will need to learn about the other. For example, the recreation center's teen club members are excited about an oral history program, but they have never worked with older people. And the residents of the senior residence whom they will interview need to know what to expect from the youth. Similarly, the staff at both the recreation center and the senior residence have agreed to serve as on-site staff for the project, but they only know the age group they usually work with.

For detailed plans for preparing staff, volunteers, and participants, see the guides listed in "Program Manuals" in the Resources appendix and in the bibliography.

VOLUNTEERS

ACTIVE ELDERS

- 43% of people 55-74 years old do volunteer work an average of 5 hours per week.

- 42% of older adult volunteers work with community services (like libraries!)

Much library programming is dependent on volunteers to augment library and other agency staff. Since the recruitment and retention of volunteers is a topic of its own, and beyond the scope of this volume, a few words to the wise will suffice.

First, it is essential that volunteers be selected carefully. The best approach is to treat volunteer selection as you would the hiring of a paid staff member. Have a job description and success indicators prepared for discussion with each potential volunteer. Make it clear to all volunteers that they are expected to do the assigned tasks successfully or that they will be released from the position. See the sample volunteer application forms and position descriptions in Figures 6-1 through 6-4.

Second, be sure that volunteers are well trained in their assignments and that they are carefully managed. Most problems with volunteers arise when they are not well trained; most problems between paid staff and volunteers stem from a lack of clear supervisory channels.

Next, integrate volunteers into program staff as much as possible. Keep them informed and make them feel part of the team. This may include inviting them to the annual staff party or encouraging them to use the staff lounge.

Finally, reward volunteers for their contributions. Although they are not paid, volunteers must be valued and acknowledged. Sometimes a tangible reward is offered; for example, tickets donated by the local theater or free reserves on library books. More often, recognition is given in the form of letters, certificates, and annual awards ceremonies. One personal approach is a birthday card or gift to each volunteer from the program.

According to the video *Intergenerational Programs: Bringing the Ages Together*, successful volunteer programs have the following points in common:

1. Volunteers are sensitively matched and placed
2. Staff and volunteers are appropriately prepared and trained
3. Volunteer feels a sense of belonging
4. Volunteer feels she or he has continuous support
5. Contributions of volunteer are recognized on a regular basis
6. Program allows the volunteer the opportunity for growth and change
7. Enthusiasm for the program is evident among all involved
8. Program has continuous evaluation; concerns of volunteers or staff are acted on quickly.

FIGURE 6-1   Read Together Volunteer Application Form

READ TOGETHER
VOLUNTEER APPLICATION FORM

DATE:_____ NAME:_____

ADDRESS:_____

PHONE: HOME_____ WORK _____

AGE: (Circle one):   15-17,   18-25,   26-35,   36-45,   46-55,   56-65,   66+

STUDENT: SCHOOL_____
EMPLOYED: BUSINESS_____ OTHER_____

EDUCATION: (Circle last year completed):   1   2   3   4   5   6   7   8   9   10   11   12
College: 1   2   3   4   Graduate work _____ Degree_____

VOLUNTEER EXPERIENCE:_____
_____
_____

Have you ever worked with children? _____ If so, please explain: _____
_____
_____

State clearances for criminal and child abuse records are required for all Read Together volunteers. The total
cost is $20.00 (can be covered by program if necessary). Do you already possess current clearances? _____
If not, are you willing to apply for these clearances if you become a volunteer? _____
_____

Why do you want to be a volunteer reader? _____
_____
_____

In what ways do you think READ TOGETHER can benefit you? _____
_____
_____

In what ways do you think READ TOGETHER can benefit a child? _____
_____
_____

How did you hear about the READ TOGETHER program?_____
_____
_____

Special skills or interests:_____
_____

Restrictions or concerns:_____
_____

FIGURE 6-1 *Continued*

AVAILABILITY: (Check each that is applicable)

_____ once a week   _____ twice a week   _____ more

_____ Morning   _____ Afternoon   _____ Evening

_____ Monday   _____ Tuesday   _____ Wednesday

_____ Thursday   _____ Friday   _____ Saturday

Are you available year round?   _____ yes   _____ no
If not, please explain: _____
_____

Would you be available on short notice to substitute for another volunteer? _____

Preferred age of child: _____ 3-6   _____ 7-10   _____ no preference

Please check at least two sites where you would be willing to meet with a child:

_____ East Liberty Library   _____ South Side Library
_____ Homewood Library   _____ Knoxville Library
_____ Allegheny Regional (Northside)   _____ Mt. Washington Library
_____ Hill District Library   _____ Oakland Library

Do you have use of a car? _____   Are you able/willing to use public transportation? _____

Would you be willing to volunteer for BEGINNING WITH BOOKS in other ways, if needed? _____
If so, please check each appropriate category:

_____ recruitment of volunteers   _____ mass mailing
_____ promotion   _____ fund-raising efforts
_____ special events   _____ office work

Please give two references other than family members:

1._____
      Name   Relationship   Telephone

2._____
      Name   Relationship   Telephone

❖❖❖

I am willing to participate in the four hour READ TOGETHER training program offered by Beginning with
Books.   _____ yes   _____ no

Following my participation in this training program, I am willing to be a READ TOGETHER volunteer for at
least six months.   _____ yes   _____ no

Signature: _____   Date: _____

Please return this completed form to: Beginning with Books
                                               The Carnegie Library of Pittsburgh
                                               Homewood Branch
                                               7101 Hamilton Avenue
                                               Pittsburgh, PA 15208

FIGURE 6-2   Book Buddy Profile

Read-Aloud Partners Program

BOOK BUDDY PROFILE

Name: _____

Address: _____

City _____ Zip _____

Phone: _____

1. Do you enjoy being with children?   _____

   If so, with what age child are you most comfortable?   _____

2. Have you been a babysitter?   _____

   Did/do you enjoy it? _____

3. Have you ever read to your younger brothers or sisters?   _____

   What was their favorite book?   _____

4. What is you all-time favorite book?   _____

5. Do you recall any very special books from your childhood?   _____

   _____

6. Have you read these books?   Circle those you've read.

   Where the Wild Things Are   Curious George   Good Night Moon

   Madeline   Charlie and the Chocolate Factory

7. How would you grade your reading-aloud skills?   Circle your rating.

   Excellent   Good   So-so

8. When was the last time you read-aloud to anyone?   _____

   Did you enjoy it?   _____

9. What are you currently reading for enjoyment?

   _____

10. Why do you think you will be a good Book Buddy?

   _____

FIGURE 6-3   Grandparents Volunteer Aids Description

GRANDPARENTS AND BOOKS
Grandparent Volunteer Aide Description

A "Grandparent Volunteer Aide" is a volunteer "Library Grandparent" who has attended the three trainings and volunteers to take a more involved and extended role in helping to strengthen the GAB program by improving communications between the library and library volunteers.

Length of responsibility is six months, but may vary according to each branch's needs and can be arranged on a rotating basis with other volunteers.

Branches are encouraged to enlist a "Grandparent Volunteer Aide" if they believe it will strengthen their project and be of assistance to them.

The "Grandparent Volunteer Aide" is especially recommended for GAB branches with Children's Librarian vacancies and no Children's Library Aide.

The schedule and time commitment is to be determined by each Children's Librarian and/or Branch Librarian and their "Grandparent Volunteer Aide."

<u>Suggested Duties</u> (Duties may be changed according to branch's needs. Please consult with the GAB office when considering assigning extra duties.)

1. **Assist in organizing branch GAB meetings with Children's Librarian and Library Grandparents.***

    a. Consult and set up agreed upon date with Children's Librarian.
    b. Telephone and verify volunteers' attendance for the meetings.
    c. Record minutes of the meetings to be distributed to absent volunteers and to the GAB office.
    d. Gauge the "Library Grandparents" experiences of the program.

2. **Assist in recruiting more GAB volunteers.**

    a. Assist and coordinate distribution of flyers to local clubs, churches, senior centers, schools and other organizations.
    b. Speak about the GAB program to organizations upon the Children's Librarian's request.

3. **Assist in generating community support** - e.g. enlist Friends Group, council representation and/or other organizations.

4. **Aid in tabulating GAB monthly statistics.**

5. **Assist with scheduling "Library Grandparents"** - finding a substitute "Library Grandparent" when one calls in sick, etc.

6. **Maintain and update the puppet and flannel board collection and other materials used by "Library Grandparents."**

7. **Assist with GAB displays and bulletin board.**

8. **Assist with GAB mailing for branch** - *e.g. Get Well cards, etc.*

* *Or Branch Librarian or assigned Librarian when there is a Children's Librarian vacancy.*

Page 41

FIGURE 6-4　Description of Volunteer Responsibilities

B
U
D
D
I
E
S

DESCRIPTION OF VOLUNTEER RESPONSIBILITIES

PARTICIPATING HOSPITALS :

California Pacific Medical Center, California Campus
California Pacific Medical Center, Pacific Campus
Kaiser Hospital of San Francisco
Mount Zion Medical Center
St. Lukes Hospital
San Francisco General Hospital
University of California San Francisco Medical Center

COMMITMENT:
1. Must be willing to commit 3 hours per week.
2. Must make a one year commitment to the project.

HEALTH REQUIREMENTS
Must acquire immunizations and meet all standards of
health screening required by hospital.

UNIFORM:
Will purchase and wear a uniform if required by hospital.

TRAINING:
1. Will attend all training and orientation sessions
required by hospital or the Library.
2. Will attend Library in-service training programs.

AGE REQUIREMENTS:
Must be 16 years of age or older.

OTHER REQUIREMENTS:
1. Meets specific guidelines, rules and regulations of
hospital.
2. Follows appropriate hospital procedures, including
checking in with person in charge of unit
coordination.
3. Notifies supervisor if unable to come at designated
time due to illness, etc.
4. Gives supervisor advance notice (minimum two weeks)
of vacations and other leaves of absence.

DESCRIPTION OF DUTIES:
Volunteer reads aloud or tells stories and poems to
individual or small groups of children to entertain them
and introduce them to the world of children's literature
using preselected library materials. Puppets, finger puppets
and felt boards can be used as support materials.

- 7 -

When volunteers work with children or work in a restricted environment (e.g a nursing home), security clearances may be required. It is best to talk with the administration of the agency involved to understand their regulations. Some libraries check too with their legal counsel regarding the necessity of police and other clearances. For example, the state of Washington requires a criminal records check on any volunteer who will be working with children. Each volunteer fills in a short form which is sent to the Washington State Patrol which checks to see if the person has ever been convicted of a crime involving children. When the check has been completed, a copy of the report is sent to the agency and to the volunteer.

The legal department can also advise you on liability coverage for volunteers. Note that some national programs (e.g those sponsored by ACTION) provide insurance coverage for volunteers they place.

Note that a new federal program has been established by the National Community Service Act of 1990. Under this new law, an American Conservation and Youth Corps will be developed to provide service in "nursing homes, hospices, senior centers, hospitals, *local libraries,* parks, recreational facilities, child and adult day care centers..." [emphasis added]. Schools and community groups can apply to develop community-based projects; student volunteers will receive vouchers for educational benefits. See the Resources appendix for contact information.

OLDER ADULTS AS VOLUNTEERS

Many intergenerational programs use older adults as volunteers. Usually, this strategy allows the older person to be both participant (as the older member of the intergenerational pair) and staff. For example, in the highly successful *Grandparents and Books* program which originated at the Los Angeles Public Library, senior volunteers are taught how to read and tell stories, to use puppets and flannel boards, etc. These "grandparents" then work at a neighborhood branch on a regular schedule, sharing books with children intergenerationally. A sample flyer is shown in Figure 6-5.

Older adults are available for volunteer work because people are retiring at younger ages. Over 75 percent of people now retire before they are 65 years old. Sixty-five percent of men aged 55 to

FIGURE 6-5 Sample Grandparents and Books Flyer

GRANDPARENTS AND BOOKS

WHAT IS
GRANDPARENTS AND BOOKS?

Grandparents and Books is a State Funded community-based Library Program in which older adults volunteer to read stories to children in the Public Library. Community volunteers are given training in selecting and presenting Children's Books, in using puppets, flannel boards, and other special techniques.

You can identify the Library Grandparents by their large Grandparents and Books Volunteer button!

Children of all ages are welcome to have a Grandparent read to them while they are visiting the Public Library.

If you would like to become a Library Grandparent, or have your child participate in our program, please contact the Children's Librarian at your local Public Library.

◆

Funded by the California State Library under the Library Services and Construction Act.

42% of older adult volunteers work with community services like libraries.

64 still work; only 15 percent of men over 65 still work; the rest are retired. In fact, the ranks of retirees are swelling so fast that the U.S. Department of the Census projects that by 1992 there will be one retiree for every three workers.

These retirees are also living longer—they have an average of 13.6 years of retirement activities. Is it any wonder that *Cities Rated Almanac* now includes "opportunities for volunteerism" as a factor?

Most retirees do volunteer work. More than 70 percent of Americans 55 or older (38 million people) contribute the equivalent of at least 20 million full-time workers, according to a 1991 survey conducted by Louis Harris & Associates and sponsored by the Commonwealth Fund. Furthermore, over six million more wish to volunteer.

Nearly half of the senior volunteers work with community services, like libraries. Twenty percent specifically request work with youth. It is clear that a large pool of older adult volunteers is going untapped by libraries.

Older volunteers can be found in numerous places, including:

- Local volunteer agency
- Governor's Office of Voluntary Services
- Retired Senior Volunteer Program (RSVP)—a project of ACTION
- American Association for Retired Persons local chapter (Note that the national AARP has a computerized Volunteer Talent Bank which links prospective volunteers 50 years and older with organizations seeking their assistance; see Resources appendix for contact information)
- National Association of Retired Federal Employees (NARFE) local chapter
- Service Corps of Retired Executives (SCORE)—a project of the Small Business Administration (see *Resources* appendix for contact information)
- Retired Teachers' Association (RTA) local chapter—a program of AARP
- Service organizations
- Gray Panthers local chapter (their motto is "Age and Youth in Action")
- Alumni associations

Note that the Retired Senior Volunteer Program (RSVP) is one of three Older American Volunteer Programs under ACTION, a federal program. The program provides RSVP volunteers with insurance coverage and with reimbursement for their transportation costs. Since 1988, RSVP has had a special Intergenerational Library Assistance Project. (See the Resources appendix for contact information.)

In addition to these sources of volunteers, don't forget about the programs which *pay* older people to work with community projects. For example, the Windsor Public Library (Connecticut) has a "Library Grandma" paid by the Foster Grandparent Program. In 1989, 30,000 elders were paid by the program to work with 70,000 children. Foster Grandparents is another program of ACTION (see Resources appendix for contact information).

Another source for paid, temporary senior staff is the Senior Community Services Employment Program, also known as Title V because of its location in the Older Americans Act of 1965. This program is administered by contract agencies throughout the country; to find the agency nearest you, contact your Area Agency on Aging (see Resources appendix).

Older volunteers—and paid workers—are known for their dependability, high motivation, conscientiousness, responsibility, and skills.

7 PUBLICITY

Since most intergenerational programming is not open to the public, but is planned for specific groups of people, publicity may not seem to be a concern. However, publicity may be necessary to recruit participants (see above) or to remind participants of upcoming activities.

Avoid the common pitfall of advertising library-sponsored events only in the library. What about people who don't use the library?

If you are working with a group of people in a closed environment—a school or a nursing home—publicity is fairly simple. Strong, striking posters and a press release for their in-house newsletters may be all you will need. See Figures 7-1 through 7-3. If you want to reach independent individuals, however, it is necessary to know where the target population gets its information. Is there a free weekly that is popular with young adults in your community? Is there a senior magazine with high circulation? Do the parents of preschoolers usually attend the annual summer camp preview?

Studies of older adults report that the following are the most important vehicles for reaching them:

- Public service announcements on radio and TV
- Announcements through church and synagogue bulletins
- Large print fliers and brochures
- Posters at senior centers and other meeting places.

Posters or flyers should also be posted at "ageless" locations around the community—the laundromat, the grocery store, the bulletin board outside the post office.

For all age groups, word of mouth is a most effective promotion method. Be sure that participants in other library-sponsored programs and all library staff know about the intergenerational project. Provide flyers at your circulation desk for people to bring to friends and relatives who may be interested. And have your program partners send word-of-mouth messages through their participants and staff.

Many program planners report that a reminder postcard or telephone call is invaluable in keeping attendance high at a long-term program.

A final word: don't forget to employ the in-library methods already in place. For example, have your monthly book exhibit focus on materials with an intergenerational theme, or adult and

FIGURE 7-1 Sample Poster

DO YOU LIKE CHILDREN?
DO YOU ENJOY READING?

Seattle Public Library is looking for senior volunteers to be part of its new, intergenerational reading program, **Rock 'n Read**.

Reading and role models are important to kids.

With Rock 'n Read, Seattle Public Library is setting up special storytimes in neighborhood libraries when senior citizens and children can come together to read aloud and share favorite stories.

Rock 'n Read is coming to a community library near you and <u>we need senior readers</u>.

We will provide training, a comfortable chair and plenty of books to choose from. We'll ask you to spend 30 - 60 minutes a week reading and sharing stories with children.

Are you interested in becoming a volunteer reader?

Would you like more information?

**Please call
Debi Westwood
Rock 'n Read Coordinator
(206) 386-4673**

 Seattle Public Library

FIGURE 7-2   Sample Poster

Read Aloud Programs for the Elderly

Seattle Public Library has received a one year grant to train community volunteers to read aloud to small groups of residents in nursing homes.

We are searching for volunteers who have a love of reading, skill in reading aloud and a desire to share those interests and skills with elders who can often no longer read on their own. Volunteers would visit nursing homes on a regular basis and present one hour long programs once or twice a week. We would ask for a three month commitment to the project.

Interested? Call: **Seattle Public Library**
Volunteer Manager
625-4862
or
Mobile Services
425 Harvard Ave. E.
625-4913

Seattle Public Library

5/86150, 5-2
Read Aloud Programs for the Elderly is made possible by funds from the Library Services and Construction Act, Title I funds.

FIGURE 7-3   Sample Poster

YOUNG AND OLD TOGETHER

SATURDAY, MAY 30 10:30-1:30

THE CALUMET CITY PUBLIC LIBRARY AND YOUTH AND FAMILY
SERVICES WILL BE SPONSORING A VERY SPECIAL PROGRAM,
"YOUNG AND OLD TOGETHER--GENERATIONS TOUCH." GIRL
SCOUTS AND BOY SCOUTS OF THE AREA WILL BE GATHERING
TOGETHER LOCAL HISTORY STORIES TOLD TO THEM BY THE
OLDER, LOCAL RESIDENTS. VIDEO TAPES OF THESE EVENTS
AND PLACES, SUCH AS LOCAL CHURCHES, SANDRIDGE NATURE
CENTER, THE FIRST POST OFFICE ETC. WILL BE SHOWN.
ALL RESIDENTS, YOUNG AND OLD, ARE INVITED TO THIS
PROGRAM. REFRESHMENTS WILL BE SERVED BY THE SAME
YOUTH THAT GATHERED THE STORIES.

PLEASE REGISTER

Calumet City Public Library
660 Manistee Avenue
Calumet City, Illinois 60409

862-6220

children's books written on the same topic. Another approach is to use your display cases to illustrate intergenerational concerns. For instance, have a photography contest which calls for pictures of oldsters and youngsters reading together and display all entries in the library.

EVALUATION

There are many approaches to evaluation including written surveys, oral self-report, and interviews. Whichever form is chosen, be sure to evaluate the program from each distinct perspective: the older adult participants, the youth participants, the host agencies, the library, and the community. These differing client populations necessitate different evaluative methods.

If more than one agency is involved, different protocols must be met and more than one approach to evaluation may be needed. Remember, too, that the method of evaluation depends on its purpose. If the evaluation is required by the funding source, the approach may be considerably different than if the point is to assess whether participants are pleased enough to warrant continuing the program.

Here are some questions, adapted from Tom Bird of Far West Labs, that the library and its partners should ask themselves.

- Are people being brought together for meaningful activity?
- Is the activity mutually beneficial? Are there rewards for all participants?
- Does the program promote understanding across generations?
- Does the program have a strong community base?
- Could this activity become a tradition in time?
- What are the indicators of success?

9 OBSTACLES

The savvy program planner anticipates potential problems and plans their solutions early. When asked to name expected obstacles to intergenerational programming, four items are consistently mentioned by participants in workshops throughout the country: lack of funding, potential abuse of children by older volunteers, the difficulty of choosing a program which will appeal to varied ages, and staffing. Staff of intergenerational programs consistently name the following two major obstacles: transportation and scheduling. In this section, these six concerns will be addressed.

FUNDING

In a time of decreased funding for public libraries, this is a real concern—and not just for intergenerational programs. Because intergenerational issues and approaches are considered innovative and are attracting attention, however, funding sources are available.

The Library Services and Construction Act (LSCA) was amended in 1990 to include intergenerational programs as a priority for Title I funds. Because of this, some state library agencies, for example Ohio, have rewritten their own long-range plans to include intergenerational initiatives. Contact your state library agency for information on how to apply for an LSCA Title I grant and on the availability of state funds.

In 1989, the National Community Service Act authorized a new federal program to assist local services. One of its components is support of intergenerational programs. Contact the Commission on National and Community Service or your local office for information (See Resources appendix).

Another federal program which may assist with volunteers is the current Domestic Volunteer Service Act which expands the Older American Volunteer Program in 11 areas including programs "that provide adult and school-based literacy assistance" and those "that provide before-and after-school activities that are sponsored by organizations such as libraries, that serve children of working parents." Also specified are "intergenerational library literacy programs" (Domestic Volunteer Service Act, PL 101-204).

Local organizations often fund intergenerational projects, too. Contact your Junior League, alumni organizations, and service associations such as Rotary and Seroptomists. Don't forget the Friends of the Library.

If you do not have the time or inclination for grant writing or fund raising, reconsider the idea of agency partners. Perhaps you can cooperate with a wealthier agency or with an organization which has its own funding ideas or grant writers. Or reconsider your initial program idea. Can it be accomplished without additional funds? Again, the partner agency may be key—does it have the materials which the library lacks and the program needs? Often programs can be done with no cash outlays. Remember, too, that it is often easier to get donations of items (e.g, art supplies, film, food) than of money. One or more local businesses may donate the supplies needed in exchange for the publicity the program will provide.

CHILD ABUSE AND OTHER SECURITY ISSUES

Although this is often raised as a concern, no library programs have reported abuse problems using senior volunteers with children. In most places, no security checks are done for library volunteers. In other communities, police clearances are done in special circumstances. In Delray Beach, Florida, for example, the police department and the Department of Motor Vehicles cleared all volunteers in the Palm Beach County Library/West Atlantic Branch homework help program, because the volunteers were driving children from school to the library in their own cars. The state of Washington requires a criminal records check on any volunteer working with children. This, however, is most unusual. The vast majority of intergenerational programs are done in the context of a larger program. For example, the nursing home hosts the program; nursing home staff attend and monitor the program. Or older volunteers help latchkey children in the library; the library is open for public use and library staff is present.

The Los Angeles Public Library's Grandparents and Books program reports no security problems with any of its 280 volunteers in 30 branches. To ensure the safety of the children involved, each Grandparent wears a special identifying button which the children are taught to recognize. In addition, photographs of the Grandparents—with information on the days and hours they are available—are posted in the branch.

If your administration or a host organization is concerned about security issues, it is best to check with the library's legal counsel on regulations and responsibilities.

CHOOSING AN INTERESTING PROGRAM

It is possible, of course, for any program to be a failure. It may be that the upcoming election is not as interesting a topic as the planners supposed (or that it's a topic which has received too much attention already). Although there are no guarantees for success, a well-selected planning committee and one or more enthusiastic partners are your success insurance.

As discussed earlier, a planning committee for intergenerational programming should include representatives of all the ages involved. They are the most knowledgeable about what is interesting enough to appeal to participants. The project partners also represent the needs and interests of the groups you plan to engage.

In addition, the partner agency may provide the participants themselves so that attendance is not a concern. For example, if the local history society and the elementary school are partners with the library in a local history program, participation by the older historians and by the young students is already ensured.

If the library is planning to organize an intergenerational program alone—perhaps a storytelling marathon—the library should work with an advisory committee, do a simple community assessment of the likelihood of interest, and stress publicity in the planning. One easy approach is to use a tried-and-true program idea such as those described in the next section.

STAFFING

One of the advantages of intergenerational programming in the library is that it opens up the possibility of cross-departmental cooperation. The children's department (or the older adult specialist) does not have to work alone. Existing staff works together, thereby minimizing the need for additional staff.

Again, working with another agency can be invaluable. Their staff and your existing staff can work together, again minimizing the need for more.

Volunteers, as discussed in chapter 6, are often used to augment in-house staff in intergenerational programming. Remember, though, that paid staff will be needed to recruit, train, supervise, and recognize volunteers.

TRANSPORTATION

Because many intergenerational programs happen outside the library building, and/or with participants from various locations, transportation is often a necessary component. Libraries rarely provide (or fund) the transportation themselves; this is one element usually left to a partner or contributor who already owns vehicles and employs drivers. There are likely to be many such agencies in your community, e.g, school systems, meals-on-wheels, senior centers, and children's daycare programs.

If it is not possible to use another agency's vehicles, it is best to contract out for transportation so that safety and liability questions are addressed professionally. A local merchant or service group might fund such a contract if their name is painted on the side of the vehicle providing publicity all around town.

SCHEDULING

Arranging your program on the right day at the right time and place can be difficult. Please see the scheduling section in chapter 5 for suggestions.

On the next page is a generic planning worksheet and action plan. Please see specific worksheets for each program model in *Part Three: Program Models.*

WORKSHEET 9-1

GENERIC INTERGENERATIONAL PROGRAM PLANNING WORKSHEET

Program Idea:

Program Title:

Target Month/Year:

Target Audience:

Mutual Benefits:

Whose Cooperation at Library is Needed:

Whose Approval at Library is Needed:

Possible Partner Agencies:

Contacts at Agencies:

Possible Advisory Committee Members & Who They Represent:

Sources for Participants & Contact Names:

Library Resources Available:

Other Materials/ Supplies Needed:

Possible Sources for Materials/ Supplies:

Funding Needed:

Possible Sources for Funding:

Additional Staffing Needs:

Possible Sources of Paid Staff:

Possible Sources of Volunteers:

Location for Program:

Transportation Necessary? Possible Sources:

Scheduling for Program:

Lifespan of Program:

Potential Obstacles:

Proposed Solutions:

How will program be evaluated?

Other Comments:

WORKSHEET 9-2

GENERIC INTERGENERATIONAL PROGRAM ACTION PLAN

Program Title: _____

Program Date & Time: _____

Program Location: _____

Number of Participants Expected: _____

Person(s) Responsible: _____

	Person Responsible	Target Date	Date Done
In-House Approval:			
Partner Agencies Contacted:			
Advisory Committee Convened:			
Young Participants:			
Older Participants:			
Preparation of Participants:			
Paid Staff Needed:			
Volunteers Needed:			
Preparation of Staff (Paid & Volunteer):			

	Person Responsible	Target Date	Date Done
Materials/Supplies:			
Funding:			
Equipment:			
Space:			
Transportation:			
Publicity:			
Refreshments:			
Reports:			
Evaluation:			
Follow-Up:			
Other:			

PART III
PROGRAM MODELS

In preparation for this book, an exhaustive search of the literature was done. Then a simple survey form was sent to all of the library-based intergenerational programs mentioned. Surveys were also sent to the few libraries who had responded to the national study done in 1991 by the Illinois Intergenerational Initiative and to any libraries identified through the professional grapevine. All told, 99 programs were queried; 61 responded or were reached by telephone.

It turned out that a number of programs which sounded especially interesting in the descriptive article or book chapter never existed. They had been ideas—usually on grant applications—which had not come to fruition. These are not reported in this section which covers only real programs whose existence could be verified.

Numerous successful programs no longer exist. As the original director moves on, as libraries close their doors permanently, as agencies renegotiate responsibilities, and as funding sources change, programs—even wonderful intergenerational ones—disappear. Some of these projects are mentioned here with their current status noted.

This section of the book highlights exemplary, innovative intergenerational library-based programs with which the author was able to make contact. Many others exist (which the author would like to know about—see survey form following Preface). Still other excellent programs take place outside of libraries—and could easily be adapted to libraries—but only a few of these are covered here.

10 ONE-TIME PROGRAMS, ANNUAL EVENTS, AND SPECIAL PROJECTS

The third week in May is National Intergenerational Week!

One way to start small is to mount a one-time program or a special event. Below are successful examples of this approach.

Note that special events are often scheduled for holidays or commemorative weeks; for an intergenerational programming calendar (see chapter 5).

SHARE THE MAGIC

Pekin (IL) Public Library

An annual Christmas program for grandparents and grandchildren, started in 1987 and repeated every year since, *Share the Magic* combines entertainment (e.g, magician, clown, ventriloquist), refreshments (popcorn and punch), and the creation of a special holiday card. A Polaroid photograph is taken of each intergenerational pair. This picture and a handprint of the child are attached to a card which has space for the child to request a "magic wish," something special she or he wants to do with the grandparent. Local merchants, such as Walgreen's Drugs and K-Mart, donate the film, college students take the photos, and staff and volunteers serve refreshments and assist in other ways. The major expense is hiring an entertainer; Joan Wood, the librarian, reports that she has been able to get 30 to 45 minute programs for $50 to $75. Preregistration of participants is required.

This program has been so successful that it spawned a similar summer version in 1988, *Remembering Summertime*, which featured the child's silhouette (rather than photos and handprints) and lists by both grandchild and grandparent of favorite childhood summertime games and toys. Another spinoff program, in 1991, was *Send A Story*. The library videotaped grandparents, grandchildren, friends, or relatives reading a short story; the videotapes were then sent to a loved one living far away. Participants preregistered and brought their own blank videotapes.

This library has other, long-term intergenerational programs, described elsewhere in this chapter.

GRANDPARENTS' AWARD FOR BEST PICTURE BOOK

Fletcher Free Library (Burlington, VT)

In 1988, the outreach librarian, Suzi Wizowaty, convened a panel of judges made up of residents of a local nursing home. They

61

met weekly to evaluate 25 picture books pre-selected by the librarian and to select two for their award. The judges were honored with champagne, flowers, and certificates and both the library and a local bookstore displayed the winning titles and the judges' names. Based on this successful project, the next year it was expanded to include judges from other nursing homes and elementary schools. Unfortunately, the program was discontinued when the librarian left.

The Allerton Public Library (Monticello, IL) had a similar project in 1980. The children's librarian took children's books to nursing homes. Residents then read the books and filled out simple review forms. Selected reviews were integrated into library-produced bibliographies distributed to library patrons.

GRANDPARENTS TEA

Shaker Heights Public Library (OH)
Grandparents Day 1992 was celebrated in the library with stories and refreshments. According to the librarian, Margaret Simon, "this was a very easy program to run. It was low cost, only the cost of refreshments, and had high interest."

GRANDPARENTS DAY STORYTIME

Roselle Public Library (IL)
The Roselle Public Library celebrated Grandparents Day in 1992 with a special preschool storytime. Books with an intergenerational theme were read and a puppet show and art project were shared. Refreshments (donated by the parents) were served and each grandparent was given a carnation, courtesy of a local florist. Another donor supplied needlepointed canvases in hearts and bears for each pair. The library plans to continue this as an annual event.

The Morgan Hill Public Library (CA) also had a special preschool story time for Grandparent's Day in 1980. The publicity instructed children to bring a grandparent to the library to hear stories about grandparents.

GRANDPARENTS' DAY OPEN HOUSE

Escondido Public Library (CA)
An annual event held the Friday preceding Grandparents' Day, the Library Open House lasts 90 minutes and includes displays, videos, a craft table, bookmarks, gifts (usually items from the

summer reading program such as pencils), and refreshments. Each intergenerational pair is also given a simple oral history interview form with questions about the grandparents' schooling, family, clothes, entertainment, work, etc. Each year attendance has grown since this was first held in 1984, reports the librarian, Candace Cameron.

BINGO AND OTHER INTERGENERATIONAL ACTIVITIES

Calumet City Public Library (IL)
An annual intergenerational activities day was held at the library for a number of years (but since has been discontinued due to staff changes). Craft projects, story times, and bingo games were offered. Youth services staff worked with volunteers from a local senior citizens organization to plan and implement the program.

VALENTINES FOR NURSING HOME RESIDENTS

Briggs Lawrence County Public Library (OH)
In 1992, library director Margaret Reid initiated a project for children (aged three to 12) to create valentines for residents of six county nursing homes which receive library services. The children made the cards in the library, using book jackets and magazine pictures as well as construction paper and doilies. The cards were then delivered by the extension librarian.The program was so successful that she plans to repeat it each year and to offer more intergenerational programs on topics such as calligraphy and sports card collecting. Her advice to others: "Evaluate your library's strengths and the community's needs. Start small—you can always grow!"

A similar project in Mountain View (California) in 1980 had children make valentines for residents of convalescent homes; the valentines were then delivered on the bookmobile's regular route.

GIVING THANKS FOR GRANDPARENTS

Sacramento Public Library (CA)
On Thanksgiving day, 1991, the Del Paso Heights branch of the Sacramento Public Library invited grandparents and grandchildren to a one-hour program at which they made picture frames, had a picture taken while reading a story together, and saw the film *What Mary Jo Shared* while enjoying refreshments. This library

Certainly the highlight of this program was fostering family communication, but there are other rewards: the preservation of oral history, promotion of storytelling, encouraging children's writing skills, and circulation of books.

has other, long-term intergenerational projects, described elsewhere in this chapter.

SHARING FAMILY STORIES

Oak Lawn Public Library (IL)

In 1986 the library offered a special program in celebration of Grandparents' Day. Children in grades four through eight were invited to come with a grandparent. After the librarian, Cynthia Dobrez, gave a book talk and told family stories of her own, grandparents were encouraged to tell a family story one-on-one to their grandchildren; these stories were then written down and illustrated by the children. Dobrez states "Certainly the highlight of this program was fostering family communication, but there are other rewards: the preservation of oral history, promotion of storytelling, encouraging children's writing skills, and circulation of books. Now each child has a book of their grandparent's story to share with their own children and grandchildren." Publicity was done through flyers to teachers, the senior citizen's centers, the library's information desk and newsletter, and ten local newspapers. Preregistration was required.

STORYTELLING FESTIVAL

Elmhurst Public Library (IL)

Every year before the fireworks begin on the Fourth of July, people gather on the lawn of the library for a storytelling festival. Over the years, it has developed into an intergenerational program with storytellers and listeners of many ages.

BIRTHDAY CLUB

Mid-York Library System (NY)

Children who came to the library with a parent or grandparent to register for library cards during 1988 were included in the library's birthday club. The library sent each child a birthday card which was redeemable at the library for a free book.

CHILDREN'S BOOK WEEK

Seneca Public Library (IL)

On Thursday, November 19, 1992, 28 eighth grade students from the local middle school came to the public library to read to

FIGURE 10-1   Family Stories Flyer

Family stories are very precious and should not be lost. The Library is encouraging the development of the tradition of family story telling by celebrating September Grandparents Day with a special program.

Sharing Family Stories

After hearing a family story told by Librarian Cindy Dobrez, grandparents will relate a family story to their grandchildren. Together they will write and illustrate a book to preserve the story. They will hear about other ways to preserve family stories such as with quilts, buttons, books and other devices.

This program is for grandchildren in grades four through eight who will be accompanied by their grandparents.

Friday, September 19
3:30 p.m. to 5:00 p.m.

Registration begins Monday, September 8, either in person or by phone.

 OAK LAWN PUBLIC LIBRARY
9427 SOUTH RAYMOND AVENUE
OAK LAWN, ILLINOIS 60453
(312) 422 4993

20 preschoolers. The students had prepared—they had practiced reading children's books and some had gathered props—at school before they came to the library. Project director Jill Ames reports that "It was a very successful example of how the public school and the public library can work together."

WORKSHEET 10-1

ONE-TIME PROGRAMS PLANNING WORKSHEET

Program Idea:

Holiday/Special Event Tie-In:

Program Title:

Target Audience:

Mutual Benefits for Participants:

Whose Cooperation at Library is Needed:

Whose Approval at Library is Needed:

Possible Partner Agencies:

Contacts at Agencies:

Possible Advisory Committee Members & Who They Represent:

Will Participants Be Recruited Individually? If so, How?

Will Participants Be Invited in Groups? If So, Which Groups? Contact?

Library Resources Available:

Other Materials/Supplies Needed:

Possible Sources for Materials/Supplies:

Funding Needed: (See budget sheet)

Possible Sources for Funding:

Additional Staffing Needs:

Possible Sources of Paid Staff:

Possible Sources of Volunteers:

Program Date & Time & Length:

Location for Program:

Transportation Necessary? Possible Sources?

Potential Obstacles:

Proposed Solutions:

How Will Program Be Evaluated?

Other Comments:

WORKSHEET 10-2

ONE-TIME PROGRAMS BUDGET SHEET

Items	Projected Cost	Source of Funds
Publicity:		
Craft Supplies/Materials:		
Miscellaneous Supplies (e.g, name tags):		
Equipment:		
Audiovisual Equipment:		
Entertainment:		
Refreshments & Paper Goods:		
Other:		

WORKSHEET 10-3

ONE-TIME PROGRAMS ACTION PLAN

Program Title: _____

Program Sponsors: _____

Program Date & Time: _____

Program Location: _____

Number of Participants Expected: _____

Person(s) Responsible: _____

	Person Responsible	Target Date	Date Done
In-House Approval Received:			
Partner Agencies Contacted:			
Advisory Committee Convened:			
Paid Staff:			
Volunteers:			
Preparation of Staff (Paid & Volunteer):			
Participants Invited:			
Participants Prepared:			

	Person Responsible	Target Date	Date Done
Materials/Supplies:			
Funding:			
Equipment:			
Space:			
Publicity:			
Transportation:			
Refreshments:			
Cleanup:			
Follow-up (e.g, thank yous to volunteers)			
Reports:			
Evaluation:			

STORY AND READING PROGRAMS

Sharing stories or reading are naturals for intergenerational programs. Besides being clearly library-related (and thereby easiest to sell if colleagues are reluctant), storytelling and reading are familiar to all age groups and condescending to none. These programs can be offered in the library or off-site, in simple to complex forms, usually with little cash outlay.

In this chapter, programs held in the library (on-site) are discussed. See chapter 18 for off-site story and reading programs.

GRANDPARENTS AND BOOKS
Los Angeles Public Library

In 1987, the Children's Services Department identified two needs and one solution. "The need of LA's elderly population (nearly one-third of whom live alone) to find meaningful contact with others, and the need to promote the love of reading in the over 200,000 LA children who have no one to care for them after school and who have among the lowest reading scores in California. By bringing the two together and training older adults to read to the children, two positive results were expected: reading skills would be bolstered and intergenerational understanding and appreciation could be enhanced."

The idea is a simple one—on specified days (weekly) in designated branches, volunteer Library Grandparents are available to read to children and to share reading activities such as puppet shows. The children come to the library individually (not in scheduled groups) and the volunteer reads with as many children as happen to come whether a small or large group.

A pilot program of Grandparents and Books was begun in three branches in 1988 with an LSCA grant. By the end of 1989, 46 Library Grandparents had read 1,966 hours to over 7,061 children in three locations. Two and a half years later (June 1992) the LAPL program had 400 volunteers who had read nearly 34,000 hours to more than 80,000 children in 52 branches. Grandparents read in Chinese, Korean, Spanish, Russian, Hebrew, and French as well as in English.

This program has been so successful that the California State Library assisted 76 libraries in FY1991 and 60 more in FY1992 to replicate it. All totaled, the State Library has now funded 188 library sites for *Grandparents and Books*. In addition to awarding $5,000 collection development grants, the State Library has sponsored workshops for library staff who receive grants, and developed publicity materials to recruit volunteers and participants.

The backbone of the program has been its careful selection and training of volunteers. Besides conventional publicity—flyers,

FIGURE 11-1   LAPL 'Library Grandparent' Flyer

press releases, public service announcements, displays—library staff makes recruitment speeches at community group meetings. Once selected, the volunteers are trained in three sessions, each three hours long. The first workshop starts with an introduction to the program and discussions on "Why to Read to Children" and "How to Read to Children." Then flannel board storytelling is demonstrated and volunteers make their own flannel figures. Volunteers are given a homework assignment on reading stories or using flannel boards. The second workshop starts with volunteers reading aloud in small groups and receiving feedback. A demonstration of how to select appropriate books for each age and a discussion of children's book genres follows. Last, the use of puppets is demonstrated and volunteers are shown how to make simple puppets. Another assignment is given. The last workshop starts with a tour of the library and a second chance to practice reading aloud, using a flannel board or puppets. Volunteers are then taught about library regulations and guidelines and volunteering schedules and responsibilities. Children's Story time, led by a librarian, is observed and discussed. Finally, buttons and certificates are handed out by the head librarian and refreshments are served. Follow-up, city-wide workshops for Grandparents are held quarterly.

The library is careful to recognize the Grandparents with birthday and holiday cards and thank you letters. They report that they still have some of their original Grandparents who have now been volunteering for five years and that the heaviest drop-out rate for volunteers is during the first four months. A recent survey of all the Grandparents found that 98.4 percent are satisfied with the program.

In 1993, the LAPL Grandparents and Books announced a new spinoff. The Library Grandparents will carry special bookmarks with them to be stamped each time a child is read to; when the child has at least two stamps he/she will receive a free paperback book to keep, autographed by the Grandparent.

Note that *Grandparents and Books* supersedes an earlier intergenerational program at the Los Angeles Public Library. *Project Story*, developed in the late 1970s, taught senior volunteers to tell stories in local public libraries.

An excellent Trainer's Manual is available from Bessie Egan, Consultant, California State Library, 1001 6th Street, Suite 300, Sacramento, CA 95814-3324.

ROCK 'N READ

Seattle Public Library

> By bringing the two [the elderly and school aged children with poor reading scores] together and training older adults to read to the children, two positive results were expected: reading skills would be bolstered, and intergenerational understanding and appreciation could be enhanced.

In 1991, the Seattle Public Library adapted *Grandparent and Books* for their system. In *Rock 'n Read*, senior volunteers read to children in eighteen branch libraries on a weekly basis. The "rock" part of the title comes from the signature rocking chair (with teddy bear and rug) in each participating branch. All volunteers are screened and attend a two-hour orientation. The project director, Debra Westwood, feels that the sharing between generations, and the respect it generates, is one of the high points of the program. She quotes a volunteer who states that the program offers her "the best parts of grandparenting without the fuss."

READ-TO-ME GRANDMA-PA

Belleville Public Library (KS)

This summer program, planned to coincide with the Summer Library Reading Program, matches individual children with volunteer grandparents. The children—kindergarten through third grade—are enrolled by their parents. The library matches each child with a volunteer who reads to the child one hour per week for several weeks. Besides reading stories, the child writes and compiles a book of his or her own. The librarian, Leah Krotz, reports that the two-year-old program whose stated purpose is "to develop good library habits and a love for books, while establishing a relationship with a person of another generation" is "worthwhile, special, meaningful, and fun."

FOSTER GRANDPARENTS

Windsor Public Library (CT)

Similar to the programs described above, the Wilson Branch has a Library Grandma to read to children and to assist them with their homework. The federal Foster Grandparent program pays a stipend to her for her 20 hours per week at the library. The branch manager, Gaye Rizzo, advises "You won't be disappointed [with intergenerational programming]. We've tended historically to segregate people by age. A more holistic approach is much more natural, and better received."

Other "homework helper programs" in which senior volunteers assist children with their assignments after school exist in many libraries including Pike County Library (Ohio), Westchester Library System (New York), and Redwood City Public Library (California).

STORY AND READING PROGRAMS **77**

GREAT BOOKS

Payson Public Library (AZ)

Great Books discussion programs have been offered by public libraries since the 1930s. But in 1992 the Payson Public Library sponsored an intergenerational Great Books series for teenagers and older adults. The director, Edward P. Miller, reports "Both the senior citizens and the high schoolers thoroughly enjoyed the program. The discussions were exciting—both groups participated with each other as if there were no generation gap." The program is scheduled to be repeated each semester.

HMONG FOLKTELLING PROGRAM

Sacramento Public Library (CA)

The Del Paso Heights Branch Library is a participant in the "Grandparents and Books" program. In addition, Sharyn Bate, the librarian there, has initiated a number of other intergenerational programs, including one specifically for the Hmong immigrants.

She reports:

> A five session program this past (1992) summer targeted the Hmong community. Adults told Hmong folk tales to the children in Hmong. Women from the community prepared— and let the children help prepare—food from that culture. The children then prepared plays, puppet plays, or a book based on one of the folk tales. Seven older adult men told the folk tales, eight women provided the ethnic refreshments, and 39 children participated in the plays, assisted by 16 helpers ranging in ages from 12 through 29. This was truly a multi-generational program as well as multicultural. While the focus was on the Hmong community, we had assistants from the African-American and the Caucasian communities.

She points out that, in addition to all of these volunteers, "it is imperative to establish a link with the community who will be the liaison, the coordinator, the interpreter."

Bate explains "The Hmong Folktelling Program was designed so that the children retain a pride and a link with their culture. . . . Watching the faces of the men as they told their stories, and the faces of the other adults as listened with the children showed the

---

Both the senior citizens and the high schoolers thoroughly enjoyed the program. The discussions were exciting—both groups participated as if there were no generation gap.

pride and strength of their culture. The children were the same as children from all cultures. They sat so quietly and respectfully during the stories, and then really cut loose during the refreshments and the puppet and book making. At times I did feel like a ringmaster at an eight-ring circus. But our final program when they invited their families to see the plays and puppet shows was delightful. . . . It was a resounding success."

GENTE Y CUENTOS/PEOPLE & STORIES

Newark Public Library (NJ)
From 1987 to 1989, Hispanic high school students and senior citizens met in the library to hear and discuss contemporary Latin American short stories in Spanish. Because some of the older adults did not read, the story was read aloud to the entire group before the discussion, led by a facilitator.

Originally begun as a pilot project to coincide with Hispanic Heritage Month in 1987, and funded by the New Jersey Committee for the Humanities, the program continued in the library for an extra year with funding from the New Jersey State Library. Although *Gente and Cuentos* programs had been established in eight sites in New Jersey, this was the only library location. The program has continued support from the Committee for the Humanities and has expanded to more locations in New Jersey and Connecticut, but is no longer centered in the library. The library, however, has assisted some of the other locales with materials and bibliographies.

Ingrid Bethancourt, the Ethnic Services Librarian who was also the project coordinator, reports that arranging for the teenagers to be released from high school during the day once a week for six weeks was not the problem she had anticipated. Instead, arranging for the older adults' participation was difficult. To make attendance easy, two meetings were held at the Senior Citizens center, two at the central library, and two at Casa Mia, a senior residence where the majority of the older participants live.

BOOK BUDDIES

Crestline Public Library (OH)
Each summer since 1984, carefully selected students from the elementary school's remedial reading program have met with an adult volunteer tutor in the library at least one-half hour per week. The child reads to the volunteer who then helps him or her to select

and check out a book to read at home. An average of 30 children register for the program each summer; sufficient volunteers are recruited through newspaper publicity. The program's success is reflected in parents and teachers' comments on the children's improvement when school re-opens in the fall. In addition, says coordinator Nancy Smithr, the "young people and adults form a friendship."

A similar program, called *Reading With A Friend*, was held for a number of summers in the 1980s at the Bucyrus Public Library (Ohio) but has since been discontinued.

READING ROUNDUP

Thomas Crane Public Library (MA)

At the Adams Shore branch in Quincy, Massachusetts students and volunteers are paired also. But in this case they meet weekly during the school year. First and second grade students in the Chapter I reading program in local elementary schools come to the public library for weekly meetings with senior volunteers. An average of 15 to 20 children have been registered each of the five years the program has been running. They are given free bus passes from the after-school daycare center to the library. A similar number of volunteers have been recruited and trained. They use a special read-aloud collection as well as books from all sections of the library. The library director, Ann McLaughlin, describes the program as very successful and "such an easy thing for libraries to do."

COMMUNITY AND SCHOOL VOLUNTEER PROGRAM

Palm Beach County Library (FL)

A similar program was held at the West Atlantic Avenue branch library in Delray Beach, Florida. The library—in conjunction with a nearby elementary school with disadvantaged children—developed this program in response to requests from older patrons to work with the school children who use the library every day after school. The school selected two children per class, recommended by teachers as those who could most benefit from the one-on-one experience, and parents signed permission slips. The volunteers were recruited by the library, screened by the school, and cleared by the police. The school then did the "matchmaking."

Each volunteer picked up her or his child at school. The two of them came to the library together for an hour or so where the

The program was very successful and "such an easy thing to do."

volunteer introduced the child to the library and its resources, helped with homework, and played games. The volunteer then drove the child home.

In 1989, after the program was in existence for five years, the school expanded its site and incorporated the program into its existing tutoring program. The public library is no longer involved.

LIBRARY GRANDMA

San Benito County Library (CA)

In the early 1980s, the San Benito County Library in Hollister, California had a similar program. In that case, 17 Library Grandparents worked with children in the library on Saturdays during the school year and Monday through Friday over the summer. Stationed at a special summer reading program table, with a large "Library Grandparent" sign, these volunteers talked with children about books and reading, helped them select and locate materials, and played games. One Library Grandparent (from the Foster Grandparent program) served as coordinator for the others.

Unfortunately the entire San Benito County Library was closed in early 1993 due to lack of funding.

NOW AND THEN SUMMER READING PROGRAM

South Bay Cooperative Library System (CA)

During 1980 and 1981, the eight member libraries of the South Bay Cooperative Library System (SBCLS) held an intergenerational summer reading program. An older adult patron suggested the idea; a planning group of librarians, seniors, parents, and children met; a theme (heritage sharing) was selected; and an LSCA grant was received. An advisory committee which included children's and adult services librarians, library patrons, parents, seniors, and representatives from community agencies was convened. Among other tasks, such as developing evaluation forms, they sponsored a contest for a name; *Now and Then* was chosen.

Most of the eight libraries held weekly story hours as part of *Now and Then*. At the San Benito County Library, senior volunteers read at their weekly story times. Older adults told stories about their childhoods at a weekly *The Way It Was* series at the Palo Alto Library. At the Mountain View Public Library, the children's librarian read *Favorite Fairy Tales My Mother Told Me* to an intergenerational audience. At others, preschool and bedtime story hours were devoted to stories about grandparents.

Many of the libraries also offered special programming to supplement the system-wide reading club. These ranged from crafts programs to fashion shows to folk dancing. Often senior volunteers *were* the program. For example, the Sunnyvale Public Library had a toy-maker demonstrate old-fashioned toys and teach the children to make them. Another time they had members of the antique auto club bring their cars and talk about them. Full descriptions of these programs, and tips on using older adults as program resources, are in the manual.

Another component of the SBCLS umbrella project was a series of workshops to train staff to think intergenerationally. As a librarian at the San Jose Public Library noted "Implementing [intergenerational programs] requires focus and commitment. It requires changes in attitudes and a different approach to program planning. Since most libraries have staffing problems, a high level of enthusiasm is needed to implement new ideas successfully." The three workshops—on brainstorming, on aging, and on working with children and seniors together—addressed these needs.

The project director, Marilyn Green, writes "The intergenerational reading program was most successful at libraries where librarians were enthusiastic and positive about the idea. The program was also successful in libraries with small program audiences and a casual atmosphere. Libraries which expect large audiences at programs and where staff had less time to encourage intergenerational interaction did not report the same success. . . .Developing an intergenerational program of any kind will take time and patience. It takes time for word to get around and for friendships to grow. Librarians at libraries where such a program has worked feel it's worth the effort. You will really be taking steps to change society—from an age-divided, compartmentalized society into one where older people are welcome and valued for what they have to offer."

The manual, entitled *Intergenerational Programming in Libraries* by Marilyn Green, includes program descriptions, resource lists of all kinds, sample publicity, and detailed staff training workshop outlines. It is available from the South Bay Cooperative Library System, 25 Tower Road, San Mateo, CA 94402.

GENERATION TO GENERATION

Pekin Public Library (IL)

Pekin Public Library regularly offers a series of intergenerational activities under the banner *Generation to Generation: Adults and Kids Together*. Offered on Saturday afternoons, they range from quilting demonstrations, storytelling, crafts, and naturalist activities.

RAP PROGRAM

Union City Branch of the Alameda County Library (CA)

The Read Aloud Partners (RAP) program was started in September 1992 with an LSCA grant which targeted services to Latino residents. Based on a program at the Santa Clara Public Library (which has been temporarily discontinued pending announcement of funding), RAP organizes and trains high school students to read to children in the first through fourth grades. The pairs meet once, twice, or three times per week at the public library.

The younger children are signed up for RAP by their parents who have heard about it through the branch staff, the library newsletter, or from preschools where the librarians publicize it after regular story hours. The teens are recruited from the high school across the street from the library where the librarians do Young Adult (YA) book talks. At this particular school students must perform 20 hours of community service to graduate, so finding the volunteers is not difficult. During the summer, one high school student volunteered for 100 hours; he coordinated the other volunteers.

The teen volunteers are given a four-hour training session in the library. They are taught about volunteer responsibility as well as specifics on reading aloud and using the specially developed read aloud collection in the library. After the training, each student signs a contract with the understanding that the school will be notified of their work at the library.

During the first school year of the program, 40 teens read to 40 youngsters. In the summer months these numbers rose to 50 pairs. The library plans to make this an annual summer program from now on.

Linda Harris, the Branch Manager, reports that RAP is "wildly successful as evidenced by happy mamas, happy older students, and happy young students." She points out that the program teaches the younger children that reading can be a fun social interaction while it increases the self-esteem of the young adults.

Y/READERS

Wilmette Public Library (IL)

Teenagers in Wilmette have been reading to younger children, too. In the Y/Readers program, junior high school students read to small groups of children ages three to six on Saturday mornings. Lyn Persson, the project director, reports that the student volunteers are "enthusiastic, resourceful, and independent." The program has been ongoing since 1990.

A GRAND PAIR OF READERS

Missouri State Library

A statewide program sponsored by the State Library from 1990 to 1991, *A Grand Pair of Readers* was ingeniously simple. A pair (grandparent and child) signed up at the local public library and received a special activity folder which included bookmarks, a bibliography of children's books with an intergenerational theme, and an activity wheel (Figure 11-2). The wheel listed five starred activities and 13 others. Participants were instructed to do all the starred activities and as many as desired of the others. When an activity was completed, that section of the wheel was colored in; when all the selected activities were competed, the wheel was returned to the librarian who designated the participants as *A Grand Pair of Readers* and awarded a prize.

The starred activities were: sing a song together, draw/paint a picture about a book you read together, read a book together, play a game together, and play-act together from a story you both like. Other suggested activities included: make a musical instrument and play it, ask the librarian to help you discover something new, make two puppets and give a show, and write a story about just the two of you. Slogans for the program were "The Library Is A Grand Place" and "It's Grand to Read."

The activity folder and publicity items included artwork by James Stevenson who has since done the drawings for the American Library Association's intergenerational program publicity materials.

A Grand Pair of Readers travelled to Illinois in 1992. The Roselle Public Library reproduced the Missouri materials and used them during Children's Book Week. Grand Pairs had to include one person 50 or over and one person ten or younger. All the pairs who completed the six required activities were invited to a Gala at the end of the month. Refreshments were served, two Bi-Folkal kits were used for entertainment, and a display was mounted of the pictures made by participants.

REDISCOVER READING

Beatrice Public Library (NE)

This program is similar to the *Grand Pair of Readers* program. Each month, a new activity sheet is given to teams (consisting of

A Grand Pair of Readers

© James Stevenson. 1993

Activity Folder

★ Sponsored by the Missouri State Library
and your local public library

FIGURE 11-2 Grand Pair Activity Wheel

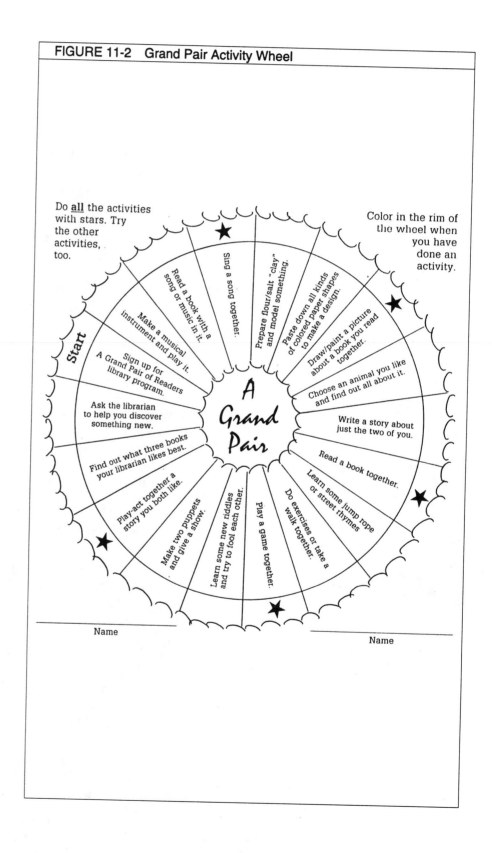

Do **all** the activities with stars. Try the other activities, too.

Color in the rim of the wheel when you have done an activity.

Start

A Grand Pair

Sing a song together.

Read a book with a song or music in it.

Make a musical instrument and play it.

Sign up for A Grand Pair of Readers library program.

Ask the librarian to help you discover something new.

Find out what three books your librarian likes best.

Play-act together a story you both like.

Make two puppets and give a show.

Learn some new riddles and try to fool each other.

Play a game together.

Do exercises or take a walk together.

Learn some jump rope or street rhymes.

Read a book together.

Write a story about just the two of you.

Choose an animal you like and find out all about it.

Draw/paint a picture about a book you read together.

Paste down all kinds of colored paper shapes to make a design.

Prepare flour/salt "clay" and model something.

Name _____

Name _____

one child and one adult) who register at the library. If they complete the three starred activities and three of the remaining seven activities, they receive a prize. The prizes are donated by different businesses each month. For example, the prize for December 1992 was a free movie rental at Econofoods.

The three-starred activities for December 1992 were current library cards for all family members, two library visits during the month, and at least five 15-minute read-aloud sessions with the child reading at least twice. Unstarred activities included watching *Reading Rainbow* on PBS; reading a book by a Caldecott, Newbery, or Golden Sower award-winning author; checking out a non-book library item; and attending a library program.

The Beatrice Public Library considers this a family literacy program because it encourages intergenerational family reading. For more on literacy programs, see the next chapter.

WORKSHEET 11-1

STORY AND READING PROGRAMS PLANNING WORKSHEET

Program Idea:

Who Will Read to Whom?

In-library or Off-site?

Program Title:

Target Audience:

Mutual Benefits for Participants:

Whose Cooperation at Library is Needed:

Whose Approval at Library is Needed:

Possible Partner Agencies:

Contacts at Agencies:

Possible Advisory Committee Members & Who They Represent:

Will Participants Be Recruited Individually? If So, How?

Will Participants Be Invited in Groups? If So, Which Groups? Contact?

Library Resources Available:

Will Reading/Activity Be Based on Library Materials?

Other Materials/Supplies Needed:

Possible Sources for Materials/Supplies:

Funding Needed: (See budget sheet)

Possible Sources for Funding:

Additional Staffing Needs:

Possible Sources of Paid Staff:

Possible Sources of Volunteers:

Training of Readers:

First Program Date & Time & Length:

How Often Will Reading/Activity Take Place?

Lifespan of Program (e.g, 6 months, one year, indefinite)

Location for Program:

Transportation Necessary? Possible Source:

Potential Obstacles:

Proposed Solutions:

How Will Program Be Evaluated?

Other Comments:

WORKSHEET 11-2

STORY AND READING PROGRAMS BUDGET SHEET

Items	Projected Cost	Source of Funds
Publicity:		
Books (to be read):		
Craft Supplies/Materials (e.g, flannel board supplies):		
Miscellaneous Supplies (e.g, tote bags, volunteer recognition):		
Furniture (e.g, rocking chairs):		
Audiovisual Equipment:		
Training of Readers:		
Entertainment:		
Refreshments & Paper Goods:		
Other:		

WORKSHEET 11-3

STORY AND READING PROGRAMS ACTION PLAN

Program Title: _____

Program Sponsors: _____

Program Date & Time: _____

Program Location: _____

Number of Participants Expected: _____

Person(s) Responsible: _____

	Person Responsible	Target Date	Date Done
In-House Approval Received:			
Partner Agencies Contacted:			
Advisory Committee Convened:			
Paid Staff:			
Volunteers:			
Preparation of Staff (Paid & Volunteer):			
Training of Readers:			
Participants Invited:			
Participants Prepared:			

	Person Responsible	Target Date	Date Done
Materials/Supplies:			
Rewards/Certificates for Participants:			
Volunteer Recognition:			
Refreshments:			
Funding:			
Equipment:			
Space:			
Publicity:			
Transportation:			
Cleanup:			
Follow-up:			
Reports:			
Evaluation:			

12 FAMILY LITERACY PROGRAMS

Often literacy programs are, by default, intergenerational. Most adult new readers enrolled in literacy projects are young and middle-aged adults; many volunteer tutors are older adults. However, one-third of illiterate people in America are over 60 years old; younger adults may be recruited as their tutors, creating an intergenerational component to learning to read.

Family literacy programs, on the other hand, are intergenerational by definition. Designed to break the cycle of illiteracy that plagues families, these projects work with both young and old within a family. According to Ruth Nickse and Shelley Quezada in *Community Collaborations for Family Literacy*, exemplary family literacy programs provide direct services to both the children and the adults. In other words, they teach both the parent or grandparent to read (or to improve reading skills) and teach the children to read (or give them pre-reading skills). They also teach parenting skills, and provide intergenerational activities which demonstrate the joy of reading and language.

Fortunately, there are many family literacy programs in libraries throughout the United States. Only a few are described here.

READ TOGETHER

Carnegie Library of Pittsburgh (PA)

One of the first library-based family literacy programs is *Beginning With Books. Read Together* is one of its three components, started in 1987 to respond to a stated need of adult new readers: to provide in-library childcare for children while their parents or grandparents are attending adult reading sessions. A second objective is to interrupt the common cycle of illiteracy by increasing reading interest and ability in at-risk children.

Trained volunteers read one-on-one to children ages three to 10 years old in eight branches of the library. Elizabeth Segel, a co-director of the program, reports:

> The intergenerational aspect of *Read Together* has been a gratifying part of the program. Some of our most memorable volunteers have been either high school students or senior citizens.

Volunteers, who are asked to make a six-month commitment to the program, are trained in a four-hour session. Included are an introduction to the program's philosophy and goals and to a variety of books. Then reading aloud is modeled and practiced. Finally, special activity materials (e.g, puppets, puzzles, games) are

93

shared. Each volunteer is given a copy of *For Reading Out Loud: A Guide to Sharing Books With Children* and a reference manual of ideas for volunteers to use. Currently, 89 children are matched with readers and 19 more matches are in progress.

To stress that reading is a family activity, the first *Read Together* session for each child begins with a staff member introducing all four members of the group to each other: the child, the parent (or grandparent), the child's reader, and the parent's tutor. After each 90-minute session, families are free to check out books, book-tape sets, and tape players. The children also receive three free books which they may keep and families are provided with free bus tickets to come to the library.

Beginning with Books works closely with the Greater Pittsburgh Literacy Council and Project LEARN, another adult literacy service provider.

The *Read Together* reference manual, which would be helpful to libraries wanting to establish a similar program, may be available upon request to *Read Together*, Carnegie Library of Pittsburgh, Homewood Branch, 701 Hamilton Avenue, Pittsburgh, PA 15208. *For Reading Aloud* rev. ed. by Margaret M. Kimmel and Elizabeth Segal, Dell, 1988, is available at libraries and bookstores.

FAMILIES FOR LITERACY

California State Library
One of only three statewide library-based literacy initiatives, California's Families for Literacy (FFL) provides state assistance funds to local libraries already providing adult literacy services. The idea is to expand existing programs to include direct services to the families of adult learners who have preschool children. In 1992/93 (its fifth year of operation), 32 libraries participated in the program, bringing the total of libraries who have received funds to over 100. Each local program is unique but must meet certain requirements.

Libraries with FFL funding must provide books for ownership, hold meetings in libraries to introduce families to the resources available, provide storytelling and other reading-oriented activities for the entire family (intergenerational), encourage the use of children's books and other materials in the adult literacy program, teach parents how to select books and how to read them to their children, foster a family environment for reading, and help parents gain access to books on parenting and related topics.

According to director Carole Talan, FFL is viewed as a joint effort of children's services, adult services, and adult literacy

"Our experience indicates that community partners and intergenerational concepts can instill a love for reading and learning into the children...and, hopefully, bring an end to the cycle of illiteracy."

—Denise Fischer

services in the local library. In addition, programs are encouraged to form partnerships with other agencies and organizations (e.g, Head Start, Even Start, day care providers, adult schools, homeless shelters, detention facilities, etc.) in their communities in order to better serve these families.

A video (with guidebook) about FFL is available from Carole Talan, Family Literacy Specialist, California State Library, Library Development Services, 1001 6th Street, #300, Sacramento, CA 95814-3324.

COMMUNITY COLLABORATIONS FOR FAMILY LITERACY

Massachusetts Board of Library Commissioners

In 1990 the Board received a Title VI grant from the U.S. Department of Education to develop a model for community planning of family literacy programs. Based on *Collaborations for Literacy*, the pioneering work by Ruth Nickse at Boston University, but adapted to library-specific situations, the grant project provided a framework and assistance for cooperative community efforts.

Six local teams met over a 16-month period to create a program specific to their own communities. Team members represented various social and educational services as well as the public library. Five proposals for LSCA Title I funding, two for Title VI funding, and one for Even Start funding resulted from this process.

In addition to developing their own family literacy programs, the teams documented their planning processes. The data collected was the basis for a book, *Community Collaborations for Family Literacy Handbook*, by Shelley Quezada and Ruth Nickse.

One other outcome of the project was a state-wide family literacy conference which generated 18 LSCA grant applications and a new statewide family literacy policy initiative in the Governor's Education Reform Bill of 1992.

FAMILIES READING TOGETHER

Sterling Municipal Library (TX)

Also based on *Collaborations for Literacy*, this project is a cooperative effort of the public library, the school district, the Hispanic Education Access Committee (HEAC)—a community group sponsored by the local college—and Hispanic-owned businesses. The school district provides the services of a Chapter 1 counselor and a site (an elementary school campus). HEAC recruits the volunteer tutors. The library provides materials, training of tutors, and a bilingual site coordinator. Hispanic-owned businesses contribute funds to hire a security guard for the evenings when classes meet.

In this model, four-week instructional units have been developed for each type of participant: adults, school-aged children, preschool children, and infants. Co-director Denise Fischer writes, "Our experience indicates that community partners and intergenerational concepts can instill a love for reading and learning into the children of our 'Workforce 2000' work pool and, hopefully, bring an end to the cycle of illiteracy."

FAMILY READING PROGRAM

New York State Library

In 1987-88 the New York State Library coordinated a one-year family literacy initiative with LSCA funds. As with the California initiative, libraries were required to work cooperatively with community literacy agencies. Carol Sheffer (Outreach and Literacy Consultant) and Anne Simon (Youth Services Consultant) report that 17 library systems, each with a grant of up to $50,000, designed their own programs. In all, 107 libraries in 52 counties served more than 220,000 users during the year. Programs ranged from lap-sits for at-risk families in the library to story time boxes created for loan.

AMERICAN LIBRARY ASSOCIATION/BELL ATLANTIC FAMILY LITERACY PARTNERSHIP

In 1989 the Bell Atlantic Charitable Foundation began funding a jointly sponsored family literacy project with the American Library Association (ALA). Initially, 25 public libraries in the mid-Atlantic region (Bell Atlantic's territory) were given $5,000 grants and provided with training to establish family literacy programs. As of late 1992, 62 family literacy programs in 46 community libraries in Maryland, Virginia, New Jersey, Delaware, Pennsylvania, West Virginia, and Washington, D.C. had been funded. The last round of funding was granted in March 1993 for an 18-month period. All told, $1,000,000 from Bell Atlantic will have been awarded. For more information, contact Margaret Mansour, Project Director, Bell Atlantic Family Literacy Partnership, American Library Association, 50 E. Huron Street, Chicago, IL 60611.

CARGILL/ALA PARTNERS FOR FAMILY LITERACY

Cargill Corporation and the American Library Association

Cargill Cares, a program of the Cargill Corporation, sponsors various outreach community projects. Their international family literacy initiative was launched in January 1992 in cooperation with the American Library Association. Cargill retirees and employee volunteers are developing local projects in conjunction with their local librarians and literacy groups. Exemplary projects will receive monetary prizes (totaling $100,000 in 1992 and $50,000 in 1993) from Cargill Corporation. For more information, contact Margaret Mansour, Project Director, Partners for Family Literacy, American Library Association, 50 E. Huron Street, Chicago, IL 60611.

WORKSHEET 12-1

LITERACY PROGRAMS PLANNING WORKSHEET

Program Idea:

In-library or Off-site?

Program Title:

Target Audience:

Direct Service to the Adults:

Direct Service to the Children:

Joy of Reading Component:

Parenting Skill Component:

Literacy Approach (e.g, Laubach, LVA):

Part of an Existing Literacy Program?

Whose Cooperation at Library is Needed?

Whose Approval at Library is Needed?

Possible Partner Agencies:

Contacts at Agencies:

Possible Advisory Committee Members & Who They Represent:

How Will Tutors Be Recruited?

How Will Tutors Be Trained?

Will Participants Be Recruited Individually? If So, How?

Will Participants Be Invited in Groups? If So, Which Groups? Contact?

Library Resources Available:

Will Reading/Activity Be Based on Library Materials?

Other Materials/Supplies Needed:

Possible Sources for Materials/Supplies:

Funding Needed: (See budget sheet)

Possible Sources for Funding:

Additional Staffing Needs:

Possible Sources of Paid Staff:

Possible Sources of Volunteers:

Program Starting Date:

Lifespan of Program (e.g, 6 months, one year, indefinite)

Location for Program:

Transportation Necessary? Possible Sources:

Potential Obstacles:

Proposed Solutions:

How Will Program Be Evaluated?

How Will New Readers Be Rewarded?

How Will Tutors Be Recognized?

Other Comments:

WORKSHEET 12-2

LITERACY PROGRAMS BUDGET SHEET

Items	Projected Cost	Source of Funds
Publicity:		
Books (to be read):		
Craft Supplies/Materials (e.g, flannel board supplies):		
Miscellaneous Supplies (e.g, puppets, tote bags):		
Audiovisual Equipment:		
Tutor Training:		
Awards/Certificates:		
Other:		

WORKSHEET 12-3

LITERACY PROGRAMS ACTION PLAN

Program Title: _____

Program Sponsors: _____

Program Date & Time: _____

Program Location: _____

Number of Participants Expected: _____

Person(s) Responsible: _____

	Person Responsible	**Target Date**	**Date Done**
In-House Approval:			
Partner Agencies:			
Advisory Committee:			
Paid Staff:			
Tutors:			
Training of Tutors:			
Participants Invited:			
Tutor Coordination:			
Participants Oriented:			

	Person Responsible	Target Date	Date Done
Materials/Supplies:			
Rewards/Certificates for New Readers:			
Recognition for Tutors:			
Funding:			
Equipment:			
Space:			
Publicity:			
Reports:			
Evaluation:			

13 STORY AND PROGRAM KITS

Program kits are packaged materials on a theme, for one or more specific age group. Kits can comprise an entire project or can be an introduction to other, more ambitious intergenerational programming. For libraries lacking in space and staff, program packages can be loaned to others for use elsewhere. Libraries looking for in-house programs can train volunteers to use the kits in the library where they may be used alone or as part of a larger program.

BI-FOLKAL PRODUCTIONS

A nonprofit corporation, Bi-Folkal Productions was established in 1976 by two librarians to encourage creative programming with older adults and the sharing of experiences between the generations. 16 multisensory program kits, each focusing on a single time or topic from the past, have been published and are available for rent or purchase.

Kit topics include: music, the decades, automobiles, school days, the seasons, farm days, train rides, birthdays, the fashion, county fairs, fun and games, work life, and pets. Each kit includes a wide variety of media and sensory resources including a slide/tape (or video) presentation to watch, scratch-and-sniff squares to smell, realia to feel, and music to hear (and to sing). Skits, jokes, and other program pieces are in each kit, along with a handbook which contains many other suggestions and bibliographies.

A new item, *Learning from the Past*, has recently been published to assist librarians and others in using the Bi-Folkal kits intergenerationally. This guide has a separate chapter for each program kit with curriculum connections, instructional objectives, follow-up activities, and a bibliography.

Many libraries (as well as nursing homes and other agencies) have purchased Bi-Folkal kits for in-house programming and for loan to community groups to use. For example, the Topeka Public Library (Kansas) uses the kits in their own outreach program (the *Red Carpet Service*), trains volunteers to use the kits in nursing homes and other places, and loans the kits out to groups to use themselves. The *Red Carpet Service* Manager, Jean Tevis, reports that she has had older adult volunteers, teen volunteers, and school classes take the kits into nursing homes. She has also had an older adult volunteer use the kits with fourth graders who came to the library for a special activity.

For more information on the availability of kits near you, or to rent/purchase your own, contact Bi-Folkal Productions, Inc., 809 Williamson Street, Madison, WI 53703.

Program kits are packaged materials on a theme, for one or more specific age group.

"When you do these programs, it catches your heart and you just want to keep doing them."

SENIOR STORIES
Fresno County Free Library (CA)

An LSCA-funded project, Senior Stories developed ten kits for use by Head Start and 20 local senior-centered agencies to do intergenerational programs. Each kit, designed for preschoolers through third graders, was based on a theme and included picture books with intergenerational themes and handmade puppets carefully produced to be intergenerational and multicultural as well. For example, the *Friends* kit had five picture books about friends; a copy of the *Golden Songbook*, an activity packet of nursery rhymes, finger plays, and puppet plays; five Hispanic family puppets (grandfather, mother, father, daughter, and son), a Disney songtape, and a rubber stamp with ink pad.

Staff from those agencies were trained in use of the kits and other library-owned materials (e.g, Bi-Folkal kits). In addition, the project produced a teacher's manual to encourage classroom teachers to borrow and use the kits. The project director, Karen Moore Reynolds, reports that the intergenerational aspect of the program no longer exists, but that the kits still circulate to interested groups to use as they wish.

REMINISCENCE COLLECTION

Ontario Cooperative Library System (NY)

As part of a larger LSCA-funded "Grandreading" project, the Wayne County Library System in Newark, N.Y. developed thematic boxes filled with books and related items (e.g, cassettes, puppets, puzzles, and realia) to encourage reminiscence and sharing. The "Whatsits" box, for example, has a soap saver, a feather bed fluffer, a sock stretcher, a pie crimper, and a facsimile of the 1909 Sears Roebuck & Co. catalog along with the book *Kids America* by Steven Caney. The "Automobiles" box has a model of a 1932 roadster, a Fibber McGee & Molly recording of "The Old Jalopy," and Peter Spier's *Tin Lizzie*.

The boxes are distributed to schools and to senior centers for use in intergenerational programming. For example, a fifth grade class invited seniors to tea in the school media center. The "Games" box was used by the participants to get acquainted with each other. The cost of the kits is underwritten by local corporations and foundations.

According to Nancy Rubery, Children's Consultant for the Wayne County Library System, "the most important person in organizing such a program is the coordinator who ties it all together. . . .The project coordinator's tasks are threefold: to facilitate testing of the models,. . .to accumulate materials that might generate sharing and reminiscence, and to publicize the possibility of an entirely new way of using children's literature."

PRIME TIME—BOOKS TO GO

Broward County Division of Libraries (FL)

"It fills a real void in my life. In fact, never in my life have I put in so little and gotten so much in return." So a senior volunteer was quoted in an article about *Prime Time*.

In this project, older adult volunteers, using kits prepared and loaned by the library, do library programming at 60 Title XX child care centers throughout the county. The kits include books, puppets and other program materials which the volunteers have been trained to use. They pick up the kits at ten branch libraries where the youth services librarians work with the project. Kit topics include "I love books!," "Mother May I?," "Happy Birthday to Us!," "We're very good friends, my brother and I," and "Yumm!"

Many agencies and organizations have cooperated on this program. For example, the Child Care Connection (a United Way-sponsored daycare coordinating agency) helped the library select appropriate centers, and many volunteer agencies recruited the 60 volunteers for the library. Corporations such as American Express and J.C. Penney have contributed funds.

Marlene Lee, Youth Services Coordinator, offers these words of advice to librarians considering intergenerational programming. "Do it! The rewards of involving 'oldsters' with youngsters are many including excellent public relations and media coverage and outside monies."

This exciting intergenerational program was started by the Broward County Library in 1991 using an LSCA grant; it has since been picked up by the library's general budget. The *Prime Time* coordinator, Shelly Turetzky, is part of a new department responsible for programming. She is assisted by a seasoned volunteer who coordinates the new volunteers.

A video about the project is available for loan from Prime Time, Broward County Library, 100 St. Andrews, Ft. Lauderdale, FL 33301.

GRANDPARENTS' KITS

County of Los Angeles Public Library (CA)

The Point Dume community library in Malibu is located next to a senior center. This situation led to the development of Grandparents' Kits in the late 1980s. The library loaned kits to grandparents to use when their grandchildren visited. Each kit included an audiocassette of music, a picture book, and a puppet on a related theme. For example, an elephant puppet was packaged with Mercer Mayer's *Ah-choo* and a cassette of Sharon, Lois, and Bram's *One Elephant, Deux Elephant*.

This library has been closed due to funding shortages. According to the librarian, the kits no longer exist though she reports "they were a great idea."

TOGETHER WITH BOOKS

Reading Public Library (PA)

Age-specific kits of books and other library materials are created by the library system for loan to older adults when their preschool or school-aged grandchildren are visiting, or for any intergenerational visit. Each kit includes age-appropriate books, audiocassettes, puzzles and art supplies based on a theme (e.g, family). Community support is provided by the local 4-H chapter which sews the canvas bags for the library to fill.

WORKSHEET 13-1

STORY AND PROGRAM KITS PLANNING WORKSHEET

Program Idea:

Program Title:

Target Audience:

Mutual Benefits for Participants:

Whose Cooperation at Library is Needed?

Whose Approval at Library is Needed?

Possible Partner Agencies:

Contacts at Agencies:

Possible Advisory Committee Members & Who They Represent:

How Will Potential Kits Users Be Identified? Trained?

How Will Kits Be Circulated/Maintained?

Library Resources Available:

Other Materials/Supplies Needed:

Possible Sources for Materials/Supplies:

Funding Needed: (See budget sheet)

Possible Sources for Funding:

Additional Staffing Needs:

Possible Sources of Paid Staff:

Possible Sources of Volunteers:

Target Date for Availability of Kits:

Potential Obstacles:

Proposed Solutions:

How Will Kits and Their Use Be Evaluated?

Other Comments:

WORKSHEET 13-2

STORY AND PROGRAM KITS BUDGET SHEET

	Items	Projected Cost	Source of Funds
Kit Contents:			
Kits Boxes/Bags:			
Miscellaneous Supplies:			
Publicity:			
Training sessions:			
Other:			

WORKSHEET 13-3

STORY AND PROGRAM KITS ACTION PLAN

Program Title: _____
Program Sponsors: _____
Program Date & Time: _____
Program Location: _____
Person(s) Responsible: _____

	Person Responsible	Target Date	Date Done
In-House Approval:			
Partner Agencies:			
Advisory Committee Convened:			
Paid Staff:			
Volunteers:			
Preparation of Staff (Paid & Volunteer):			
Kit Creation:			
Kit Circulation/Maintenance:			
Kit Training:			

	Person Responsible	**Target Date**	**Date Done**
Materials/Supplies:			
Funding:			
Equipment:			
Space:			
Publicity:			
Reports:			
Evaluation:			

14 PENPAL PROGRAMS

Programs that establish one-on-one relationships between people through letter writing are easy and fun. Correspondence is familiar to older adults who remember times before phone and fax, and is a favorite pastime of children from eight years old through their teens. Advantages of penpal programs are that library space is not an issue (letter writing can be done elsewhere) and that people with disabilities or that are isolated or housebound can participate. Letter writing is also an excellent activity for latchkey children, whether at home or in the library.

GRANDPARENTS AND BOOKS PENPALS

Sacramento Public Library (CA)

As part of a larger *Grandparents and Books* project (see chapters 10 and 11), the Del Paso Heights Public Library established a penpal program in January 1992. It began with 17 adults and 22 children corresponding. The youth—ranging from six through 17 years—signed up at the library which then matched them with Books-by-Mail (homebound) patrons who had expressed interest. To ensure both anonymity and security, and to avoid postage costs, all correspondence funnels through the library rather than by mail. The librarian, Sharyn G. Bate, comments "The Pen Pal program has been very rewarding for me as I see the children's faces when they see a letter in the mailbox. . . .I have seen handwriting skills improve, cognitive abilities enhanced, verbal skills improve, and self-esteem blossom. I know it has been as rewarding for many of the adults as well. Many of the Books-by-Mail patrons are housebound because of physical limitations, but they still have much to offer and the desire to feel they can still contribute. This program has given them a world beyond once again."

OTHER PENPAL PROGRAMS

Because of their simplicity, many non-library agencies have established intergenerational penpal progams. For example, ten counties in Ohio have such programs sponsored by VISTA. Penpal projects run the gamut of possibiities: elementary school children writing to nursing home residents, older children corresponding with homebound residents, girl scouts writing to young children, college students writing to seniors or to preschoolers.

For ideas to structure the first exchange of letters (or every letter, if you choose), two resources are especially helpful. *Grandletters* was designed to assist grandparents in writing to their distant grandchildren, but the materials are just as good for people who are not related. Contact *Grandletters*, Kansas State University, Cooperative Extension Service, Manhattan, KS 66506. Or borrow some of the ideas in *First Writes* by Margaret Gulsvig. Other good resources are the self-published book by Meyer Moldeven entitled *A Grandpa's Notebook: Ideas and Stories to Encourage Grandparent-Grandchild Interaction, Communication, and Well-Being*; Charles Slaybaugh's *The Grandparents' Catalog*; and *Long Distance Grandparenting: An Intergenerational Activity Book* by Jenelle and Kenneth Koftan.

WORKSHEET 14-1

PENPAL PROGRAMS PLANNING WORKSHEET

Program Idea:

Program Title:

Target Audience:

Whose Cooperation at Library is Needed?

Whose Approval at Library is Needed?

Possible Partner Agencies:

Contacts at Agencies:

Possible Advisory Committee Members and Who They Represent:

Will Penpals Be Recruited Individually? If So, How?

Will Penpals Be Invited in Groups? (e.g, schools, scouts) If So, Which Groups?

Contact?

Will Library/other agency serve as "mailbox" or will US Postal Service Be Used?

How will initial correspondence be structured?

Any meeting of penpals planned? If so, what occasion, when, where?

Library Resources Available:

Materials/Supplies Needed (e.g, stationery, stamps):

Possible Sources for Materials/Supplies:

Funding Needed: (See budget sheet)

Possible Sources for Funding:

Additional Staffing Needs:

Possible Sources of Paid Staff:

Possible Sources of Volunteers:

Onset of Program Date:

Lifespan of Program (e.g, 6 months, one year, indefinite)

Potential Obstacles:

Proposed Solutions:

How Will Program Be Evaluated?

Other Comments:

WORKSHEET 14-2

PENPAL PROGRAMS BUDGET SHEET

Items	Projected Cost	Source of Funds
Supplies (e.g, stationery):		
Postage:		
Publicity:		
Miscellaneous Supplies:		
Other:		

WORKSHEET 14-3

PENPAL PROGRAMS ACTION PLAN

Program Title: _____

Program Sponsors: _____

Starting Date: _____

Number of Participants Expected: _____

Person(s) Responsible: _____

	Person Responsible	Target Date	Date Done
In-House Approval:			
Partner Agencies:			
Advisory Committee Convened:			
Paid Staff:			
Volunteers:			
Penpals Recruited:			
Initial Correspondence Structured:			
Materials/Supplies:			

	Person Responsible	Target Date	Date Done
Funding:			
Publicity:			
Evaluation:			

 # HISTORY PROGRAMS

History projects make the most of the life experiences of older adults and the natural curiosity of young people. They introduce the concept of elders as the keepers of history and culture and of children as the future. There are many forms of history projects; oral history, local history, and living history are especially appropriate for intergenerational exploration:

- *Oral history* is the capture of elders' memories as they speak them.
- *Local history* is the exploration of the story of a specific community.
- *Living history* is the realistic portrayal of past events and activities—history is brought alive through reenactment rather than merely recounted.

All of these approaches can be used in simple or complex forms, in the library or off-site, and with any combination of ages.

FROM SHEEP TO SHIRT

Stewart Library (IA)

In 1983 the public library in Grinell, Iowa offered a one day living history event focused on the old-time processes between sheep and shirt. Older adults in the community demonstrated sheep shearing, yarn spinning, yarn dyeing, and weaving. The librarian, Jan Irving, reports that the older adults were "enthusiastic" and the children "fascinated."

LIFE BEFORE CDS AND VCRS

Atlanta-Fulton Public Library (GA)

As part of a centennial project, the library and the historical society jointly sponsored a local history project. After the research was done, a skit with music and historic slides was prepared and titled *From the Nifty Nineties to the Nintendo Nineties*. The librarian, Jean Cornn, reports that it was performed by an intergenerational troupe of volunteers in schools and at scout gatherings, with older adults in attendance as "experts."

THE DIRTY THIRTIES

Woodward Public Library (OK)

A mixture of oral history, local history, living history, and arts on the theme of the Great Depression were shared by residents of

Woodward, Oklahoma over a two-week period in May 1984. A joint effort of the Pioneer Museum, the Woodward Arts Theater, the Public Library, Senior Center, and public schools, *The Dirty Thirties* included a week's performances of *Annie*, special exhibits at the museum, daily programs at the library, senior center, and museum, and projects (such as preparing recipes and setting up a soup line) at the school.

HISTORY SHARING THROUGH OUR PHOTOGRAPHS

Michigan Council for the Humanities

Created for the Michigan Council for the Humanities in 1979, *History Sharing Through Our Photographs* (HISTOP) uses family photos as the basis of sharing local history. Older adults select the photographs which set the frame for discussion of a period, an event, a concept—all rooted in personal experience. And children prepare "photo family trees." Photographs are the tools, but the focus of the program is on intergenerational discussion. A secondary objective is the creation of an exhibit based on the photos shared. According to the Council, libraries as well as other agencies ranging from schools and museums to senior centers and summer camps have used the HISTOP model.

One particularly interesting variation is the "Family Mystery." A set of unidentified old photos is presented for discussion. Based on speculation and visual clues, the participants write creative versions of the mystery family's history before working on their own family trees.

An excellent manual on how to implement the basic program (and other coordinating activities such as the "Family Mystery") is available for purchase from the Michigan Humanities Council at 119 Pere Marquette Drive, Suite 3B, Lansing, MI 48912-1231.

YOUNG AND OLD TOGETHER—GENERATIONS TOUCH

Calumet City Public Library (IL)

In cooperation with the city's youth and family services department, the library sponsored a special oral history project in 1987. Girl and boy scouts interviewed older residents for their stories about the area. The project culminated in a live program at the public library and a videotaped tour of the places mentioned in the elders' remarks.

History projects make the most of the life experiences of older adults and the natural curiosity of young people.

BEFORE YOUR TIME

Generational Resources Exchange/Reading Public Library (PA)

The Generational Resources Exchange (see *Library As Coordinator* section in chapter 19) developed a booklet of oral history questions for young people to ask elders. The youth records the older person's answers in the pamphlet as a permanent record. Included are other related activities such as making a personal time capsule (in a shoe box) and creating a simple family tree.

Copies of the booklet are available for two-week loan from Monica Rueno-Wenrich, The Volunteer Center of Berks County, United Way, PO Box 302, Reading, PA 19603-0302.

OTHER ORAL HISTORY RESOURCES

The Oral History Center in Cambridge, Massachusetts does some of the most exciting intergenerational oral history projects. For example, in 1992 they launched a two-year project on teen violence in Roxbury. Out-of-school youth are interviewing community residents aged ten to 70 in order to document and explore the changing experience of teenage life over five generations.

For information on their programs, to subscribe to their twice yearly report *Voices*, or to purchase their print and video materials, contact The Oral History Center, 186 1/2 Hampshire Street, Cambridge, MA 02139.

Two of the many books out on oral histories may be helpful. *How to Tape Instant Oral Biographies* by William Zimmerman (1979) and *Oral History: An Introduction for Students* by James Hoopes (1979).

WORKSHEET 15-1

HISTORY PROGRAMS PLANNING WORKSHEET

Program Idea:

Oral history? Local history? Living history?

In-library or Off-site?

One-Time or Ongoing?

Program Title:

Target Audience:

Mutual Benefits for Participants:

Whose Cooperation at the Library is Needed?

Whose Approval at the Library is Needed?

Possible Partner Agencies:

Contacts at Agencies:

Possible Advisory Committee Members & Who They Represent:

Will Participants Be Recruited Individually? If So, How?

Will Participants Be Invited in Groups? If So, Which Groups? Contact?

Library Resources Available:

Will History Activity Be Based on Library Materials?

Other Materials/Supplies Needed:

Possible Sources for Materials/Supplies:

Funding Needed: (See budget sheet)

Possible Sources for Funding:

Additional Staffing Needs:

Possible Sources of Paid Staff:

Possible Sources of Volunteers:

First Program Date & Time & Length:

How Often Will Activity Take Place?

Lifespan of Program (e.g, 6 months, one year, indefinite)

Location for Program:

Transportation Necessary? Possible Sources:

Potential Obstacles:

Proposed Solutions:

How Will Program Be Evaluated?

Other Comments:

WORKSHEET 15-2

HISTORY PROGRAMS BUDGET SHEET

Items	Projected Cost	Source of Funds
Historian/Performer:		
Publicity:		
Supplies/Materials (e.g, props, costumes, foods)		
Equipment (e.g, for living history):		
Audiovisual Equipment (e.g, for oral histories):		
Other:		

WORKSHEET 15-3

HISTORY PROGRAMS ACTION PLAN

Program Title: _____

Program Sponsors: _____

Program Date & Time: _____

Program Location: _____

Number of Participants Expected: _____

Person(s) Responsible: _____

	Person Responsible	Target Date	Date Done
In-House Approval:			
Partner Agencies:			
Advisory Committee Convened:			
Paid Staff:			
Volunteers:			
Historian/Entertainer/Teacher:			
Preparation of Staff (Paid & Volunteer):			
Participants Invited:			
Materials/Supplies:			

	Person Responsible	Target Date	Date Done
Equipment:			
Audiovisual Equipment:			
Costumes/props:			
Refreshments:			
Funding:			
Space:			
Publicity:			
Transportation:			
Cleanup:			
Follow-up (e.g, thank yous to volunteers)			
Reports:			
Evaluation:			

16 THEATER AND ARTS PROGRAMS

Art and theater programs call on participants' skills which are not age-related; therefore these activities are seen as egalitarian and mutual. They can be fun for the participants and observers alike. An added bonus is the tangible product (artwork or theatrical production) which usually results. Again, these programs can be simple or complex and located in the library or off-site.

CROSS-GENERATIONAL QUILT

Shaker Heights Public Library (OH)

To decorate the new Children's Room at the Bertram Woods Branch Library, the president of the Friends group suggested a special quilt. Ruta Marino, a noted quilt artist, volunteered to coordinate the project. She selected Jack Prelutsky's poem "Children, Children Everywhere" as the theme and recruited eight-to-ten-year-olds to design and make the quilt with older adults as "facilitators" and experts. Both children and adults were asked to register for any of three sessions (two hours each day for a week). These were: fabric design and selection, sewing and piecing the quilt, and quilting. At the first session, children drew pictures based on the poem and then transferred them to cloth selected from a wide variety brought by Marino. These picture blocks formed the basis for the quilt. Children were paired with adults at each stage. Altogether it took one month to create a spectacular, colorful, and unique quilt.

The library offers a booklet about the project (see Figure 16-1). Contact: Margaret Simon, Shaker Heights Public LIbrary, 3450 Lee Road, Shaker Heights, OH 44120.

WPA QUILTS ENCORE

Generational Resources Exchange/Reading Public Library (PA)

Generational Resources Exchange coordinated a quilting project done cooperatively by the 4-H, a local nursing home, and the public library. Nursing home residents taught 4-H members to quilt, using WPA templates owned by the public library. The completed quilt was exhibited at the library as well as other community locations.

STAGEBRIDGE

Oakland (CA)

Founded in 1978 as a senior theater group, Stagebridge is now an intergenerational troupe (with actors ranging in age from 12 to

---

FIGURE 16-1   Intergenerational Quilt Project

Friends of the Shaker Library
announces
A Special Quilt Project
for
Textile Artists
ages 8 - 12
and
Adult Volunteers

Join the Friends of the Shaker Library in a very special cross-generational quilting project to celebrate the new children's wing. Under the guidance of Shaker quilt artist Ruta Marino, we will design, piece and sew a quilt to hang in the Children's Room at Bertram Woods Branch Library. Children ages 8 to 12 are invited to participate in this exciting project. Adult volunteers of all ages are welcome to help with this friendly textile enterprise.

Session I
Design and Fabric Preparation
August 3 - August 7
9:30 - 11:30 a.m.

Participants will design the quilt, select fabrics and cut the shapes to be pieced for the quilt. Adult volunteers are welcome all week and will be needed on Thursday and Friday to help with the cutting. There may also be an opportunity to take work home.

Session II
Creating the Quilt
August 10 - August 14
9:30 - 11:30 a.m.

Participants will sew and piece together the quilt top. Adult volunteers are welcome and needed throughout the week. The only skill required is the ability to thread a needle.

Session III
Cross-Generational Quilting Project
Connecting the Threads
August 15 - September 30
9:00 a.m. - 9:00 p.m.

The quilt top creation will be set up in the children's room at the library and all interested adults and children are invited to help complete the quilting.

Sign up begins July 15. Call or visit the Children's Room at Bertram Woods Branch Library to reserve your place: 991-2421

---

82) which presents plays on intergenerational themes to schoolchildren as well as in public performances. The director, Stuart Kandell, credits the public libraries in the area for helping them

locate appropriate multicultural stories and folk tales which they then script into plays. For more information (or to order their bibliography), write Kandell at 6408 Valley View Road, Oakland, CA 94611.

OTHER INTERGENERATIONAL PERFORMING TROUPES AND ART RESOURCES

These groups are not library-based but are of interest for a number of reasons. First, as community nonprofit organizations, all of them actively search for local sponsors and partners. Why not the library? Second, libraries often need local entertainment for special events, intergenerational and otherwise. Why not an intergenerational performance?

Full Circle is an intergenerational, improvisational theater troupe in Philadelphia, Pennsylvania. Founded in 1983 at the Center for Intergenerational Learning at Temple University's Institute on Aging as a vehicle to dispel myths about older adulthood, the troupe consists of ten teenagers and ten older persons who are recruited from school and senior centers annually. After a 12-week intensive training program which includes skill-building in both improvisational theater and in lifespan development, and a series of rehearsals during which material is improvised and then polished, the troupe is ready to perform. Performances are given for specially invited intergenerational audiences. A performance consist of a series of three-to-five-minute scenes that portray intergenerational conflict and are left open-ended for discussion by the audience. For more information, contact the Center's director Dr. Nancy Z. Henkin at Temple University Institute on Aging, 1601 N. Broad Street #207, Philadelphia, PA 19122.

Dance Exchange is an intergenerational group that makes dances that are related to personal experience by combining movement with improvisation and storytelling. Contact the Dance Exchange at 1746-B Kalorama Road NW, Washington, DC 20009.

Elders Share the Arts, a community arts organization for older adults in Brooklyn, sponsors has a number of intergenerational programs. "Pearls of Wisdom" are multicultural elder storytellers who tell their tales for children and for intergenerational audiences. "Living History Theater" are performances which result from "transforming memory into art." In 1992, ESTA used the Living History approach for a "Rediscovering America Festival" which was a series of intergenerational performances celebrating cultural diversity. A book on this approach to integrating life review with performing arts, *A Stage for Memory*, is available from Teachers & Writers Collaborative, 5 Union Square West, New

> Art and theater programs call on skills which are not age-related; therefore these activities are seen as egalitarian and mutual.

York, NY 10003. Or contact ESTA Director Susan Perlstein at 57 Willoughby Street, Brooklyn, NY 11201.

Sunshine Intergenerational Chorus is a project of the Juvenile Welfare Board in St. Petersburg, FL. For information, or to borrow their video *Every Age is A Good Age* contact Jack Hartman at the Board, 4140 49th Street North, St. Petersburg, FL 33709.

Youth and Elders Inter-Act is an intergenerational improvisational program of Encomium Arts, Inc. This community agency in New Jersey is the sponsor of *Autumn Stages*, a senior "lifestory theater" program founded in 1985 to combine memory, song, and dance in performance. During 1990-1991, *Youth and Elders Inter-Act* was developed as a spin-off of the earlier program. For more information, or to order their new book about *Youth and Elders Inter-Act*, entitled *Step Into My Life*, contact Dr. Roslyn Wilder, Director, Encomium Arts, Inc., PO Box 43296, Upper Montclair, NJ 07043.

Mill Street Loft is a "multi-arts center for children, adults, and senior citizens." Founded in 1981, this not-for-profit arts center focuses on intergenerational projects and issues, including storytelling, oral history, drama, choral music, and folk arts. The center is "dedicated to promoting meaningful communication and interdependence between the generations. Using the arts to 'bridge the gap,' these intergenerational programs build a renewed sense of community." For more information, contact Andrea Sherman, Intergenerational Specialist or Carole Wolf, Executive Director, at Mill Street Loft, 12 Vassar Street, Poughkeepsie, NY 12601.

Grandparents Living Theater, an intergenerational program which developed from an existing Senior Theater program in 1986, uses a combination of oral history, improvisation, and audience interaction. For more information, contact Joy Reilly, Director, Grandparents Living Theater, 51 Jefferson Avenue, Columbus, OH 43215.

Lifespan Resources is one component of the TLC (Teaching-Learning Communities) Project in Ann Arbor, MI. They publish an excellent manual on intergenerational craft projects, (e.g, woodworking, paper cutting) entitled *Lifecraft*. And try the *Foxfire* books for other ideas on crafts and living history.

WORKSHEET 16-1

THEATER AND ARTS PROGRAMS PLANNING WORKSHEET

Program Idea:

In-library or Off-site?

Program Title:

Target Audience:

Mutual Benefits for Participants:

Whose Cooperation at Library is Needed?

Whose Approval at Library is Needed?

Possible Partner Agencies:

Contacts at Agencies:

Possible Advisory Committee Members & Who They Represent:

Will Participants Be Recruited Individually? If So, How?

Will Participants Be Invited in Groups? If So, Which Groups? Contact?

Library Resources Available:

Will Activity Be Based on Library Materials?

Other Materials/Supplies Needed (e.g, art supplies, costumes):

Possible Sources for Materials/Supplies:

Funding Needed: (See budget sheet)

Possible Sources for Funding:

Additional Staffing Needs:

Possible Sources of Paid Staff:

Possible Sources of Volunteers:

First Meeting/Rehearsal/Art Program:

First Performance/Art Show Date & Time & Length:

How Often Will Activity Take Place?

Lifespan of Program (e.g, 6 months, one year, indefinite)

Location for Program:

Transportation Necessary? Possible Sources:

Potential Obstacles:

Proposed Solutions:

How Will Program Be Evaluated?

Other Comments:

WORKSHEET 16-2

ART AND THEATER PROGRAMS BUDGET SHEET

Items	Projected Cost	Source of Funds
Art Supplies:		
Other Supplies/Materials:		
Props & Costumes:		
Audiovisual Equipment:		
Entertainment:		
Fees: (e.g, royalties)		
Transportation:		
Other:		

WORKSHEET 16-3

ART AND THEATER PROGRAMS ACTION PLAN

Program Title: _____

Program Sponsors: _____

Program Date & Time: _____

Program Location: _____

Number of Participants Expected: _____

Person(s) Responsible: _____

	Person Responsible	Target Date	Date Done
In-House Approval:			
Partner Agencies:			
Advisory Committee Convened:			
Paid Staff:			
Volunteers:			
Preparation of Staff (Paid & Volunteer):			
Participants Invited:			
Participants Prepared:			
Materials/Supplies:			

	Person Responsible	Target Date	Date Done
Props/Costumes:			
Funding:			
Equipment:			
Audiovisual Equipment:			
Rehearsal Space:			
Performance Space:			
Publicity:			
Transportation:			
Cleanup:			
Follow-up (e.g, thank yous to volunteers)			
Reports:			
Evaluation:			

17 DISCUSSION PROGRAMS: HUMANITIES AND CITIZENSHIP

For teens, middle-aged adults, and older adults, citizenship programs are usually mutual learning opportunities. They are intellectually stimulating and can result in positive local or national action. They can assist older people in feeling connected and involved and can prepare a new generation of active citizens. Held in the library or off-site, citizenship programs can also involve the library with new community partners.

Humanities programs—discussions on the arts, history, folklore, ethics, and philosophy—are usually for older youth and adults also. Again, they are intellectually stimulating, but are often personal too, as people reflect on their own experiences in the light of the humanities.

BUILDING BRIDGES TO CITIZENSHIP

Close Up Foundation (VA)

A nonprofit educational organization which seeks to stimulate responsible participation in the democratic process, the Close Up Foundation sponsors numerous programs. *Building Bridges* promotes intergenerational cooperation for both civic awareness and civic action. This project is unique in that it stresses that old and young are partners (neither is "helping" the other) and it allows each independent group to set its own agenda.

Some of the resulting projects have been: a week-long government internship in Oklahoma, a discussion series on the U.S. Constitution in Maryland, and a teleconference on the national debt in Florida. Close-Up has 12 intergenerational programs in the U.S. and Guam as of March 1993.

Note that none of these programs are library-based—yet. But *Building Bridges* requires that the program convener find both sponsors and a meeting place; the library might itself be the convener, and/or the sponsor and location.

Write for more information: Todd Crenshaw, Director, *Building Bridges to Citizenship*, Close Up Foundation, 44 Canal Center Plaza, Alexandria, VA 22314 or call 1-800-232-2000.

DISCOVERY THROUGH THE HUMANITIES

National Council on the Aging, Inc.

Designed to encourage older adults to remember and explore

their past—in the context of the humanities—*Discovery Through the Humanities* is a series of ten discussion sessions focused on a single theme. The discussions are based on carefully selected anthologies published in large print and, in some cases, audiocassette. There are 13 themes, such as "A Family Album," "We Got There on the Train," "Americans and the Land," "The Heritage of the Future," and "Exploring Values." In addition to the books of readings, NCOA provides discussion guides for each unit.

Libraries have used *Discovery Through the Humanities* since its inception in 1976, sometimes intergenerationally. One of the discussion units was designed specifically for intergenerational use: *The Family, the Courts, and the Constitution*, which focuses on family law and civil liberties. Topics for discussion include the government's role in marriage, terminally ill patients' right to die, and rights of grandparents.

To order the books—and the discussion leaders' guides—contact Sylvia Liroff, Discovery Through the Humanities, National Council on the Aging, Inc., 409 Third Street SW, Washington, DC 20024.

NATIONAL ISSUES FORUM

The National Issues Forum (NIF), a project of the Kettering Foundation, is a series of community-based discussions on national topics. The goal is for each community to reach consensus on the issue at hand.

Although not created as an intergenerational project per se, NIF encourages participation by all ages and produces its discussion materials in an abridged edition (for adult new readers or reluctant high school readers) as well as in standard book and audiocassette versions.

Libraries throughout America have sponsored NIF groups as have schools, prisons, senior centers, and every conceivable sort of community agency. To give an unusual example, in September 1992 the Worthington Public Library (Ohio) cosponsored a NIF program with the Ohio State Library and the Ohio State University's public radio station. The forum discussion was broadcast live as a call-in show with Ohio's Secretary of State and 40 discussion group members in the library. Some 20 listeners joined in the discussion via radio.

Each summer NIF holds a summer policy institute and issue-framing workshop to select four issues for the following year. For 1992-93, the issues are "People and Politics: Who Should Govern?," "The Health Care Crisis: Containing Costs, Expanding

Discussion programs for teens, middle aged adults, and older adults are mutual learning opportunities and are intellectually stimulating.

Coverage," "Criminal Violence: What Direction Now for the War on Crime?," and "Prescription for Prosperity: Four Paths to Economic Renewal." For 1993-94, discussions will focus on poverty, the federal deficit, and the right to die and medical ethics; titles have yet to be chosen.

For more information, or to order materials, contact John Rye Kinghorn or Bob Daley at National Issues Forum, 100 Commons Road, Dayton, OH 45459-2777 or call 1-800-433-7834.

GREAT DECISIONS PROGRAM

Sponsored by the Foreign Policy Association, a national non-profit, nonpartisan, nongovernmental organization devoted to world affairs education, Great Decisions is a series of citizen discussions on foreign affairs. Often sponsored by the American Association of University Women (AAUW) or the League of Women Voters, Great Decision groups are also sponsored by schools, service clubs, senior centers, and libraries around the country.

Each year the Foreign Policy Association issues a paperback book on current and critical world issues. For 1993, the eight topics are "U.S. in a New World," "United Nations," "Germany's Role," "China," "Trade and the Global Economy," "Russia and the Central Asian Republics," "India and Pakistan," and "Children at Risk." In addition to the annual book, written as a basic text, and available both in print and on audiocassette, the program produces an activity book for the series and a half-hour public TV program on each topic (available on videotape).

For more information contact your local World Affairs Council office or the Foreign Policy Association, Department SS, 729 Seventh Avenue, New York, NY 10019. To order materials, write the Foreign Policy Association, Department SS, c/o CUP Services, PO Box 6525, Ithaca, NY 14851 or call 1-800-477-5836.

STUDY CIRCLES RESOURCE CENTER

A project of the Topsfield Foundation, the Study Circles Resource Center is a nonprofit non-advocacy program that promotes study circles on domestic social and political issues. Founded in 1988, it is based on the theory that our democracy needs full participation by a knowledgeable public; its goal is to make study circles a standard form of citizen education.

Unlike many of the other discussion programs, study circles do not require a scholar or a specially trained discussion leader. Five to 20 participants meet three to six times to discuss any one issue, using reading materials prepared by the Center.

Besides providing the core reading, on reproducible masters, the Center has training materials for leaders and organizers and a newsletter. For more information, write Phyllis Emigh, Study Circle Resource Center, Pomfret, CT 06258 or call (203) 928-2616.

WORKSHEET 17-1

DISCUSSION PROGRAMS PLANNING WORKSHEET

Program Idea:

In-library or Off-site?

Will an Existing Program Be Used or a New One Created?

Program Title:

Target Audience:

Mutual Benefits for Participants:

Whose Cooperation at Library is Needed?

Whose Approval at Library is Needed?

Possible Partner Agencies:

Contacts at Agencies:

Possible Advisory Committee Members and Who They Represent:

Will Participants Be Recruited Individually? If So, How?

Will Participants Be Invited in Groups? If So, Which Groups? Contact?

Library Resources Available:

Will Discussion Be Based on Library Materials?

Other Materials/Supplies Needed (e.g, special books):

Possible Sources for Materials/Supplies:

Funding Needed: (See budget sheet)

Possible Sources for Funding:

Additional Staffing Needs (e.g, discussion leader):

Possible Sources of Paid Staff:

Possible Sources of Volunteers:

First Program Date, Time, & Length:

How Often Will Discussion Be Held?

Lifespan of Program (e.g, 6 months, one year, indefinite)

Location for Program:

Transportation Necessary? Possible Sources:

Potential Obstacles:

Proposed Solutions:

How Will Program Be Evaluated?

Other Comments:

WORKSHEET 17-2

DISCUSSION PROGRAMS BUDGET SHEET

Items	Projected Cost	Source of Funds
Books:		
Other Supplies/Materials:		
Audiovisual Equipment:		
Fees: (e.g, discussion leader)		
Transportation:		
Other (e.g, certificates for participants):		

WORKSHEET 17-3

DISCUSSION PROGRAMS ACTION PLAN

Program Title: _____
Program Sponsors: _____
Program Date & Time: _____
Program Location: _____
Number of Participants Expected: _____
Person(s) Responsible: _____

	Person Responsible	Target Date	Date Done
In-House Approval:			
Partner Agencies:			
Advisory Committee Convened:			
Paid Staff:			
Volunteers:			
Preparation of Staff (Paid & Volunteer):			
Discussion Leader:			
Participants Invited:			
Books:			

	Person Responsible	**Target Date**	**Date Done**
Materials/Supplies:			
Funding:			
Equipment:			
Audiovisual Equipment:			
Space:			
Refreshments:			
Publicity:			
Transportation:			
Cleanup:			
Follow-up (e.g, thank yous to volunteers)			
Reports:			
Evaluation:			

18 VISIT PROGRAMS

Library-sponsored visits emphasize the many stages of the life cycle. Because the visit recipient is often in need of some sort of assistance, these programs which involve youth visiting older adults or vice versa introduce the concept of generations caring for one another. By definition held off-site, visits can present the library as an active community member reaching out of its own building and can incorporate people with disabilities—who may not be able to come to the library—into library activities.

In addition to the programs discussed below, see chapter 13, *Story and Program Kits* for more off-site ideas.

SIDEKICKS

Clermont County Public Library (OH)

Sidekicks: Kids and Seniors Together is a joint program of the Clermont County Public Library and the Clermont Senior Services, Inc. to foster intergenerational learning and experiences. A six-session training program for the youth (fourth through tenth grade) was held at the Williamsburg Branch Library in 1992. The Clermont Senior Services took major responsibility for the training which covered aging awareness, sensory changes, Alzheimer's disease, and role-playing of generational conflicts. Volunteering in general, and library opportunities for volunteer work, were also covered.

At the end of the training period (six sessions held over a three-week period) the young people were awarded certificates and asked to decide among themselves what project they would like to do with their new knowledge about aging. They decided to write and perform skits and readings at a local senior center.

This group of 12 to 15 young adults still meets monthly to design programs. So far they have delivered hot meals and memory boxes to homebound seniors on National Make A Difference Day (November 14, 1992) and visited nursing homes to do poetry readings and other programs periodically. Transportation is provided by Clermont Senior Services, Inc. and the food and other items are donated by local businesses. Janet Parrott, the program director, reports that four of the youths have taken on individual volunteer responsibilities as well: two as friendly visitors to homebound persons, one as a senior services volunteer, and one as a library volunteer.

BOOK BUDDIES

San Francisco Public Library (CA)

Nearly eight years ago, the San Francisco Public Library was awarded an LSCA grant to establish and administer a program

153

where volunteers read to children in the pediatric wards of the local hospitals. As of 1993, the program has 100 volunteers who each read to children one-on-one in seven hospitals.

The volunteers—about half of whom are in their 20s and 30s and half of whom are older adults—each contribute two to three hours per week. They are trained at a four-hour session at the library (offered three times a year) and then have an orientation session at the hospital of their choice. The *Book Buddies* coordinator, Katharine Gilmartin, reports that volunteers are easily recruited with the help of the San Francisco Volunteer Center and local corporations which encourage their employees to participate in good works.

During the two years of LSCA funding, 500 books per hospital were purchased. These are kept at the hospital for the volunteers to use. At this point, expenses are minimal. These include refreshments at the training sessions, reprinting of the volunteer manual, special book bags and bibliographies for the volunteers, and volunteer recognition parties. The costs of the manuals and the book bags are reimbursed to the library by the sponsoring hospitals; the other expenses are covered by the Friends of the Library. The Friends also coordinate the volunteer intake, although the coordinator and her colleagues in Children Services do the training as part of their job descriptions.

This program receives a lot of positive press because it is so heartwarming (and photogenic). It is also an excellent example of cooperation: the public library, the Friends of the Library, and the area hospitals all work together.

STORIES THAT SPAN THE AGES

Normal Public Library (IL)

Since 1986, library staff have visited local nursing homes and read stories to residents—and to children. Originally, the public was invited to bring their children for a monthly story hour but, according to Children's Services director Vivian Carter, attendance was sporadic. Now three nursing homes are visited, each once a semester, and one of three daycare centers bring their children each time. She has found that this method works well and that both residents and children are excited, happy and talkative. She suggests combining stories with fingerplays, songs, and crafts and allowing time for interaction between children and residents.

> Library-sponsored visits emphasize the many stages of the life cycle and introduce the concept of generations caring for one another.

READ ALOUD PROGRAM

Seattle Public Library

In 1986, with LSCA funds, the Mobile Services Department started a new outreach service to Seattle nursing homes. During the first year, 32 volunteers read to 3,396 residents in nine nursing homes. In addition, circulation of materials to the participating nursing homes increased by 15 percent. Over the years the project has served as many as 16 nursing homes and retirement centers, but now serves nine again. Although the goal was "to provide mental stimulation and enrichment for the institutionalized elderly and to improve access to library materials and services," it has served an intergenerational purpose as well because the volunteer readers range in age from young adult to older adult.

Volunteer selection and training are key to the ongoing success of the project. The training program has five steps. First, each prospective volunteer is given a brief orientation to the library volunteer program. Next, prospective volunteers attend a two-and-one-half-hour orientation which explains the role of the Read Aloud volunteer in the institution, the special needs of nursing home residents, and tips on how to prepare for and present a Read Aloud program. Each prospective volunteer then has an individual interview with project staff to assess his or her particular skills and abilities. This includes a ten-minute reading (three short selections) by the volunteer which is assessed by staff. If accepted into the program, the volunteer is then matched with a partner and assigned to a program. The final stage of the training is attendance at monthly in-service training workshops.

An excellent training manual, as well as a bibliography of materials to read aloud, is available from John P. Larrivee, Volunteer Services, Seattle Public Library, 1000 Fourth Avenue, Seattle, WA 98104-1193.

GRANDFRIEND READERS

Hennepin County Library (MN)

In May 1991 the Hennepin County Library, in cooperation with the Minneapolis Public Library, started an ambitious outreach program to low-income children. *Children's Readmobile*, as it is called, serves over 1,000 preschool children with visits to 81 licensed family childcare homes and special preschool programs. At each stop, children select their own books and a library staff member does a story hour. To supplement these twice-monthly visits, senior volunteers visit some of the sites on alternate weeks.

Grandfriends is a project of the Hennepin County Retired Senior Volunteer Program (RSVP). Begun in 1984, it now has over 120 older adults volunteering at preschool sites. The libraries called on Grandfriends when it established the Readmobile; so far RSVP has placed seven volunteers with the library program during the past year.

Gretchen Wronka, Senior Librarian for Children's Services, speaks enthusiastically about both the older adult volunteer readers and the library's collaboration with RSVP. "The beauty of this cooperation," she says, is that "all the hard work is done by them." RSVP does the volunteer recruitment and coordination, provides liability insurance for the volunteers, and reimburses volunteers for their expenses. The library provides its materials and monthly volunteer training sessions on how to read to children, how to use puppets and flannel boards, and how to use library resources.

STORY GRAMS AND GRAMPS

Fitchburg Public Library (MA)

Also in its second year, this LSCA-funded project recruits and trains older adult volunteers to read to children at 12 area daycare centers and preschool classes. Using library materials from a specially selected read-aloud collection, volunteers visit their assigned agency two to four times a month.

BOOKLOVERS

California Youth Authority

In 1990 the California Youth Authority received an LSCA grant to reach reluctant readers. Adult community volunteers ("Booklovers") were recruited and trained to share their joy of reading with confined youthful offenders (wards of the state) who can read, but don't. The Booklovers conduct book talks, including reading sections aloud, from books which are available in multiple copies for the wards to borrow and read in their living units.

Originally started in the Northern California Reception Center/Clinic Library (Sacramento), where the program was well received for two years, Booklovers continues at the O.H. Close School Library (Stockton). The senior librarian there, Jim Morgan, reports that the volunteers are of all ages and that "the wards love people reading brief key passages to them. Many of the kids participate in the program again and again. I feel we are truly reaching our target audience of reluctant readers."

MAYOR'S READING CORPS

Phoenix Public Library (AZ)

A project of the Phoenix Public Library, the Mayor's Reading Corps was established by the mayor—who was the first to enroll—to promote reading and volunteerism. One hundred and forty of all ages read to children in 40 locations around the city, including schools, daycare centers, and recreation centers. All volunteers attend a one hour training session and then are supervised by the project.

OUTREACH INTERGENERATIONAL PROGRAM

Cook Memorial Library (IL)

The Cook Memorial Library in Libertyville, Illinois has presented two programs at two local intergenerational daycare centers. The first "Thanksgiving at the Tappletons" was held in November 1992; "The Rainforest" was held in April 1993. In both cases, the program included a flannel board story, a craft project, music, and snacks. The project librarian, Marlene Gregory, advises "Don't expect instant acceptance by the adults or children. Do your best, but don't take any comments personally and don't get offended if some older adults fall asleep! Have a sense of humor and be flexible!"

OTHER VISIT PROGRAMS

Exemplary, non-library visit programs may serve as models, also. Contact the following organizations for information, especially on preparing children to visit nursing homes and retirement centers:

Caring for Each Other—A Way of Life is an intergenerational daycare program, combining older people and preschoolers. Students in the third and eleventh grades visit weekly for joint activities. This project, sponsored by Generations Together, has a training video and guide available. Contact Generations Together at the University of Pittsburgh, Pittsburgh, PA 15260.

Silver Threads Among the Gold is an after-school visiting program co-sponsored by the Clackamas County Area Agency on Aging (Oregon) and the Clackamas Community College. The program consists of hour-long weekly visits to neighborhood nursing homes by children ages eight to 12. The children spend the first half hour participating in crafts, games, or music with physically active residents; they spend the remaining half-hour visiting with frail residents in their rooms. This program has been the model for many others around the country. For more information, contact the program's director, Judy Sheppard, 17360 SE Ten Eyck, Sandy, OR 97055.

Community is a weekly visit program in Phoenix, Arizona which coordinates weekly visits between students and neighboring nursing home residents as part of the on-going school curriculum. The project has produced three excellent resources: *A Guide to Community* (a 118 page manual), *Community: An Intergenerational Friendship Program* (a twenty minute video introduction to the project), and *Orientation for Youth: Aging and Nursing Homes* (a 40-minute video by Judy Sheppard to prepare children aged four to 12 to visit nursing home residents). All are available from Bi-Folkal Productions, Inc., 809 Williamson Street, Madison, WI 53703.

Magic Me is a program for at-risk youth in public and private schools who do community service projects as a vehicle for self-esteem and academic motivation. One of the projects is visiting a nursing home weekly to develop one-to-one relationships. Operating in 12 states as well as England and France, *Magic Me* has received much acclaim. For more information contact the program at 808 North Charles Street, Baltimore, MD 21201.

WORKSHEET 18-1

VISIT PROGRAMS PLANNING WORKSHEET

Program Idea:

Who Visits Whom?

Program Title:

Target Audience:

Mutual Benefits for Participants:

Whose Cooperation at Library is Needed?

Whose Approval at Library is Needed?

Whose Cooperation at Visit Site is Needed:

Whose Approval at Visit Site is Needed:

Possible Partner Agencies:

Contacts at Agencies:

Possible Advisory Committee Members and Who They Represent:

Will Participants Be Recruited Individually? If So, How?

Will Participants Be Invited in Groups? If So, Which Groups? Contact?

Preparation of Visitors:

Library Resources Available:

Will Visit Activities Be Based on Library Materials?

Other Materials/Supplies Needed:

Possible Sources for Materials/Supplies:

Funding Needed: (See budget sheet)

Possible Sources for Funding:

Additional Staffing Needs:

Possible Sources of Paid Staff:

Possible Sources of Volunteers:

First Visit Date, Time, & Length:

How Often Will Visits Take Place?

Lifespan of Program (e.g, 6 months, one year, indefinite)

Location for Program:

Transportation? Possible Sources:

Potential Obstacles:

Proposed Solutions:

How Will Program Be Evaluated?

Other Comments:

WORKSHEET 18-2

VISIT PROGRAMS BUDGET SHEET

Items	Projected Cost	Source of Funds
Books:		
Supplies/Materials:		
Audiovisual Equipment:		
Transportation:		
Refreshments:		
Other:		

WORKSHEET 18-3

ART AND THEATER PROGRAMS ACTION PLAN

Program Title: _____

Program Sponsors: _____

Program Date & Time: _____

Program Location: _____

Number of Participants Expected: _____

Person(s) Responsible: _____

	Person Responsible	**Target Date**	**Date Done**
In-House Approval:			
Partner Agencies:			
Advisory Committee Convened:			
Paid Staff:			
Volunteers:			
Preparation of Staff (Paid & Volunteer):			
Participants Invited:			
Visitors Prepared:			
Materials/Supplies:			

	Person Responsible	Target Date	Date Done
Funding:			
Equipment:			
Audiovisual Equipment:			
Space:			
Publicity:			
Transportation:			
Cleanup:			
Follow-up (e.g, thank yous to volunteers)			
Reports:			
Evaluation:			

19 THE LIBRARY AS COORDINATOR

An exciting role for libraries is that of coordinator of community intergenerational programs. As information specialist, agency matchmaker, and meeting convener, the library ensures that intergenerational programs exist in the community as collaborative efforts. Without necessarily planning or providing the programs themselves.

GENERATIONAL RESOURCES EXCHANGE

Reading Public Library (PA)

An innovative model program, Generational Resources Exchange (GRE) began in 1984 as a simple collection of resources on intergenerational initiatives offered by the public library for loan to other agencies. During its seven years, GRE developed into a coordinating body—and resource collection—for many countywide activities.

As staff at both the Berks County Area Agency on Aging (AAA) and the library developed ideas for programs and cooperative efforts, a collaboration between the two agencies grew. The library provided the office space and the resource collection, and hired staff who were paid with funds from the AAA. Additional funding came from grants and additional staffing from VISTA.

Besides direct programs in the community, such as *After School Connections*, a telephone reassurance program for seniors and latchkey children, GRE provided many coordinating services including a monthly calendar of events with intergenerational program ideas. GRE also did training and published a number of excellent resources including *Before Your Time* on oral history, *Games Your Grandparents Played*, and a programming manual called *So Now What?*

In 1991, as the library closed temporarily for remodeling and the AAA's funding constricted, GRE was reduced. The collection (including the above named titles) is now housed at the Volunteer Center of Reading and Berks County, part of the United Way agency, and is available for loan. Contact Monica Ruano-Wenrich, Volunteer Center, United Way of Berks County, PO Box 302, Reading, PA 19603-302.

GRANDREADING PROJECT

Wayne County Library System (NY)

In 1987, the Wayne County Library convened a one-day workshop "designed to stimulate intergenerational sharing." Over 100 people from senior citizens groups and community agencies joined librarians to hear a storyteller and a panel discussion

165

(gerontologist, information specialist, and child psychologist), and to discuss the possibilities. At the end of the workshop, representatives of more than 50 libraries stayed to plan cooperative projects among school and public libraries. One of the outcomes was the Reminiscence Collections discussed in chapter 13.

GIVE US BOOKS, GIVE US WINGS

Jefferson County Public Library (CO)

In response to a request from the Older Adult Service and Information System (OASIS) in 1989, the Jefferson County Public Library developed a program series for the public entitled *Give Us Books, Give Us Wings: Sharing Books With Children*. Offered in the OASIS catalog of courses, the program series attracted 11 people, each of whom attended the four sessions for individual reasons. Most were older adults wanting to share books with grandchildren; one was a clown who wanted to use stories in her show; one was an older adult interested in reading at a homeless shelter.

Similar to programs the library has offered to Home Economics students, parent groups, and other local organizations, the course covered book selection, reading aloud techniques, story enhancements, and storytelling. The librarian pointed out that "Jefferson County Public Library and other . . .libraries could become an important link in community services by offering children's literature programs for older adults and providing opportunities for seniors to use their knowledge and experience."

LIFE SPECTRUM PROGRAMMING

Pekin Public Library (IL)

This is a unique LSCA project whose "mission was to establish community-wide capability for intergenerational programming with the library serving as a resource center and advisor." Begun in 1991-92, the projects included collection development, community workshops, and marketing and circulation of resources.

After a careful collection assessment—an evaluation of the library's materials which could be used as-is or adapted for intergenerational use—the collection was enriched with new materials, both print and audiovisual. Next an annotated bibliography was developed, listing print materials, videos, kits, and equipment available from the library for intergenerational use.

A library-sponsored workshop for community service providers came next. Eighty-one library directors and 82 community service

---

FIGURE 19-1   Flyer for Pekin's Intergenerational Program

GENERATION TO GENERATION

Adults and Kids Together At Pekin Public Library
Free programs, Saturdays, 2 p.m.

OCTOBER 17, 1992
"Collecting Baseball Cards" Arley Cummings from Blue Diamond Traders will tell how to get started in this interesting hobby. Bring a card to have Mr. Cummings estimate its value.

OCTOBER 24, 1992
"Fun With Halloween" Don't plan to hear scary stories, just bring favorite Halloween memories to share. We'll make some Halloween decorations to take home. If you have any plastic eggs (from hosiery) or round boxes (salt, oatmeal), please bring them along to use.

NOVEMBER 7, 1992
"Chemistry All Around Us" Susan McCormick, chemist at the USDA Northern Research Lab in Peoria will show some of the ways that chemistry affects our everyday lives. You'll be surprised!

NOVEMBER 14, 1992
"Origami Magic" Steve Richards will teach the basics of origami, the ancient Japanese art of folding single sheets of paper into shapes of animals, flowers and other objects. Learn to make some figures to take home with you or to give to a special friend!

NOVEMBER 21, 1992
"Stories For Everyone" Come and enjoy stories told by an expert storyteller. Stories will be for the enjoyment of all ages!

These programs for all ages to enjoy! This means grandparents, parents, kids, special young and older friends and neighbors. Come to one or all of them and share times to remember!

Pekin Public Library...301 S. 4th St., Pekin, IL 61554...(309) 347-7111

providers were invited; 43 community agencies and seven libraries sent representatives. Agencies included the city park district, schools, senior centers, nursing homes, Head Start, Even Start, hospital, and churches. The three-hour workshop featured speakers, a video, and a slide/tape program as well as open discussion and browsing in the collection. Joan Wood, the project director, reports "The workshop is a very practical way to reach a targeted group in order to explain intergenerational programming benefits and to display the library's collection in this area. It is also a dynamic way to promote the library's image as an information source and a community-wide information provider."

The library has marketed its collection by distributing the bibliography (*Bringing Generations Together*), displaying items from the collection, and community presentations. Now the library is tracking use of the collection and equipment to assess the project's effectiveness.

For a copy of *Bringing Generations Together* or *Life Spectrum Programming: A Community Model Plan* contact Joan Wood, Project Director, Pekin Public Library, 301 S. 4th Street, Pekin, IL 61554.

INTERGENERATIONAL ACTIVITIES COMMITTEES: ANOTHER APPROACH

Another approach to coordinating community programming is the Intergenerational Activities Committee model pioneered by the senior center in Lakewood, Illinois in 1983. It has since been replicated in a number of places, none of which are libraries.

The committee is a community-wide group of people concerned with the needs of youth and elders. A sponsoring agency (the library?) convenes the committee which establishes its own internal structure, identifies community needs for specific intergenerational programs, and establishes such programs through its subcommittees.

For more on this approach, see Catherine Ventura-Merkel and Lorraine Lidoff's *Community Planning for Intergenerational Programming* (1983), Jane Angelis' *Creating Intergenerational Coalitions* (1992), and Ventura-Merkel's *Strategies for Change: Building State and Local Coalitions on Intergenerational Issues and Programs* (1990).

PART IV
QUICK-START IDEAS

Perhaps you admire the concept of intergenerational programming in libraries, but are reluctant to start a new program. Lack of staff, lack of space, lack of funds, lack of enthusiasm, lack of administrative support—some or all of these make any new project seem impossible. In that case, try out one of the quick-start ideas below. Low cost and low risk, these approaches can introduce intergenerational philosophy to your library with a minimum of planning and a maximum of success.

- Display and use children's materials with intergenerational themes. Juvenile publishing reflects our times; intergenerational picture books are hot items. Feature these in your story hours and library displays to start discussion about intergenerational themes among your patrons and your staff members.
- Hold a joint staff meeting with both youth and adult services librarians. If your staff is too large, designate liaisons so that the channels of communication are open between age-segregated departments. Perhaps have a joint in-service training on intergenerational issues. One way or another, clear the way for cooperative interdepartmental programs in the future.
- Expand a current program intergenerationally. Two popular examples are intergenerational summer reading programs and intergenerational story hours. Or what about opening those film series and travelogue evenings so that they are aimed at youth and adults together?
- Publicize the library's wealth of resources to other agencies who will use them intergenerationally. For example, publicize your puppets and films to nursing homes as well as to nursery schools. Suggest that the preschool program which borrows library books may want to share them at the senior center.
- As new programs develop, think intergenerationally. If you hear that the library will begin a lecture series on the upcoming local elections, speak up for the intergenerational approach so that young adults are included. Or if the outreach department decides to try book discussions for homebound patrons by teleconference, suggest that all ages be involved.
- Diversify your existing library volunteers. Many libraries rely totally on retirees for volunteers. If that's true in your library, recruit younger volunteers at the local high school or college. If, however, most of your library's volunteers are

middle-aged Junior League members, recruit senior volunteers. Your volunteer program will model the concept of intergenerational activity. And you will have community members ready when you decide to convene an intergenerational advisory committee.

- Use existing intergenerational program kits. For example, the Bi-Folkal kits or the "Discovery Through the Humanities" discussion sets can be rented or borrowed inexpensively and short-term to give your library a taste of intergenerational programming.
- Share your new knowledge and enthusiasm about intergenerational programs with other staff members. Perhaps one of *them* will spearhead the intergenerational initiative in your library.

APPENDIX

RESOURCES

PROGRAM MANUALS

Angelis, Jane. *Getting Started Now: A Concise Guide to Developing Effective Intergenerational Programs.* Carbondale, IL: Illinois Intergenerational Initiative, 1990. [Anthony Hall 104, Southern Illinois University, Carbondale, IL 62901]

Arguelles, Mary and Beata Peck Little. *So Now What?* Reading, PA: Generational Resources Exchange, 1989. [Volunteer Center, Berks County United Way, Reading, PA 19603-0302]

Barkman, Donna. *Learning from the Past: Using Bi-Folkal Productions in School and Intergenerational Settings.* Madison, WI: Bi-Folkal Productions, Inc., 1992. [809 Williamson Street, Madison, WI 53703]

Becoming a School Partner: A Guidebook for Organizing Intergenerational Partnerships in Schools. Washington, D.C.: AARP, 1992. [1909 K St. N.W., Washington D.C., 20049]

Berkowitz, Lois and Beryl Lieff Benderly. *Building Bridges to Citizenship: How to Create Successful Intergenerational Citizenship Programs.* Alexandria, VA: Close-Up Foundation, 1989. [44 Canal Center Plaza, Alexandria, VA 22314]

Chandler, S. *Person to Person: A Community Service Guide for Youth Groups Visiting Senior Residences.* Kensington, MD: Interages, 1990. [9411 Connecticut Avenue, Kensington, MD 20895]

Critchell, Mary King and Jacquenette Locker. *Lifecraft: A Guide to Intergenerational Sharing of Activities.* Ann Arbor, MI: Life Span Resources, 1980. [1212 Roosevelt Street, Ann Arbor, MI 48104]

The Foster Grandparent Program: A Manual for Planning, Implementing, and Operating the Foster Grandparent Program. La Quinta, CA: Elverita Lewis Foundation, 1988. [PO Box 1539, La Quinta, CA 92253]

Friedman, S. *Closing the Gap: An Intergenerational Discussion Model Guide for Replication.* Kensington, MD: Interages, 1990. [9411 Connecticut Avenue, Kensington, MD 20895]

Grandparent Read to Me: An Intergenerational Education Program. Lakewood, OH: Lakewood City Schools, 1990. [Department of Pupil Personnel, Lakewood Schools, 1470 Warren Road, Lakewood, OH 44107]

Griff, M. *Activities for Intergenerational Programming: What Works, What Doesn't, and Why*. Canton, OH: the author, 1992. [McKinley Center, 800 Market Avenue North, Suite A, Canton, OH 44702]

Green, Marilyn. *Intergenerational Programming in Libraries: A Manual Based on the Experiences of the South Bay Cooperative Library System*. San Mateo, CA: 1981. [25 Tower Road, San Mateo, CA 94402]

Leonard, Gloria. *Read Aloud Programs: Instructional Manual*. Seattle, WA: Seattle Public Library, 1987. [1000 Fourth Avenue, Seattle, WA 98104]

McDuffie, Winifred G. *Intergenerational Activities Program Handbook*. 3d. ed. Binghamton, NY: Broome County Child Development Council, Inc., 1989. [Box 880, Binghamton, NY 13902-0880]

Melcher, Joseph. *Caring is the Key: Building a School-Based Intergenerational Service Program*. Pittsburgh: Generations Together, 1992. [University of Pittsburgh, 121 University Place #300, Pittsburgh, PA 15260]

Mersereau, Yvonne and Mary Glover. *A Guide to Community: An Intergenerational Friendship Program Between Young People and Nursing Home Residents*. rev. ed. Madison, WI: Bi-Folkal Productions, Inc., 1992. [809 Williamson Street, Madison, WI 53703]

Miller, I. and J. Moore. *Avenues of Love: An Intergenerational Activities Manual*. Willingboro, NJ: Geriatric Educational Consultants, 1991. [34 Middleton Lane, Willingboro, NJ 08046]

Older Adult and Teenage Volunteers in Service to Others. Kansas City, MO: Camp Fire, Inc., 1986. [4601 Madison Avenue, Kansas City, MO 64112-1278]

Rosen, Nancy. *The HISTOP Manual*. Lansing, MI: Michigan Council for the Humanities, 1983. [Nisbet Building #30, 1407 S. Harrison Rd., East Lansing, MI 48824]

Roumpf, Margaret Lynn. *Hand in Hand: Leader's Guide to Intergenerational Programs for Girl Scouts*. Salem, OR: Santiam Girl Scout Council, 1975. [339 Washington SE #104, Salem, OR 97302]

Sheppard, Judy. *Silver Threads Handbook*. Oak Grove, OR: Clackamas County Area Agency on Aging, 1985. [PO Box 68369, Oak Grove, OR 97268-0369]

A Time and Place for Sharing: A Practical Guide for Developing Intergenerational Programs. South Pasadena, CA: The Beverly Foundation, 1984. [70 South Lake Avenue #750, South Pasadena, CA 91101-2601]

Wade, Maureen and Susan Patron. *Grandparents and Books: Trainer's Manual.* rev. ed. Sacramento, CA: California State Library, 1991. [1001 6th Street #300, Sacramento, CA 95814-3324

COMMUNITY COORDINATION MANUALS

Angelis, Jane. *Creating Intergenerational Coalitions: Bottom-Up Top-Down Strategies.* Carbondale, IL: Illinois Intergenerational Initiative, 1992. [Anthony Hall 104, Southern Illinois University, Carbondale, IL 62901]

Quezada, Shelley and Ruth Nickse. *Community Collaborations for Literacy.* NY: Neal-Schuman Publishers, 1993.

Thorp, Kathlyn. *Intergenerational Programs: A Resource for Community Renewal.* Madison, WI: Wisconsin Positive Youth Development Initiative, Inc., 1985. [30 W. Mifflin Street #908, Madison, WI 53703]

Ventura-Merkel, Catherine. *Strategies for Change: Building State and Local Coalitions on Intergenerational Issues and Programs.* Washington, DC: Generations United, 1990. [c/o Child Welfare League, 440 First Street NW #310, Washington, DC 20001]

Wood, Joan. *Life Spectrum Programming: A Community Model Plan.* Pekin, IL: Pekin Public Library, 1992. [301 S. Fourth Street, Pekin, IL 61554]

INTERGENERATIONAL NEWSLETTERS

National

Continuance
Illinois Intergenerational Initiative
Anthony Hall 104
Southern Illinois University
Carbondale, IL 62901

Exchange
Generations Together
University of Pittsburgh
121 University Place #300
Pittsburgh, PA 15260

Grandparent's Journal
1414 E. Marietta Avenue
Spokane, WA 99207

Interchange
Center for Intergenerational Learning
Temple University
1601 North Broad Street
Philadelphia, PA 19122

Linkages
Center for Understanding Aging
Framington State College
Framingham, MA 01701

Newsline
Generations United
c/o Child Welfare League
440 First Street NW #310
Washington, DC 20001-2085

Vital Connections: The Grandparenting Newsletter
PO Box 31
Lake Placid, NY 12946

Cultural Connections
Elders Share the Arts, Inc.
57 Willoughby Street
Brooklyn, NY 11201

Regional

Continuity
Secondary Schools Intergenerational Program
City School District of New Rochelle
515 North Avenue
New Rochelle, NY 10801

Intergenerational Clearinghouse Newsletter
Wisconsin Intergenerational Network
PO Box 5171
Madison, WI 53705

Kinnections
Kansas Intergenerational Network (KIN)
PO Box 47054
Topeka, KS 66647

Interages News
Montgomery County Intergenerational Center
9411 Connecticut Avenue
Kensington, MD 20895

MINews
Massachusetts Intergenerational Network
PO Box 2152
Framingham, MA 01701

Newsletter
Generations United of Michigan
29100 Northwestern Highway
Southfield, MI 48034

NYSIgN Newsletter
New York State Intergenerational Network
2 Lafayette Street, 15th floor
New York, NY 10007

Let's Link Ages in Virginia
Northern Virginia Community College
3001 Beauregard Street
Alexandria, VA 22311-5097

WIN Newsletter
Wisconsin Intergenerational Network
PO Box 5171
Madison, WI 53705

STATE INTERGENERATIONAL NETWORKS/ COALITIONS

California
Northern California Intergenerational Network
4032 Maker Street
Napa, CA 94558
(707) 255-5430

Southern California Intergenerational Network
Center for Community Education
Office of Los Angeles County Superintendent
9300 East Imperial Highway
Downey, CA 90242
(213) 922-6356

Colorado
Colorado Intergenerational Network
1430 North Hancock
Colorado Springs, CO 80903
(719) 473-6335

Illinois
Illinois Intergenerational Initiative
Anthony Hall 218
Southern Illinois University
Carbondale, IL 62901
(618) 453-1186

Kansas
Kansas Intergenerational Network
PO Box 47054
Topeka, KS 66647
(913) 266-2491

Massachusetts
Massachusetts Intergenerational Network
PO Box 2152
Framingham, MA 01701
(508) 626-4978

Michigan
Generations United of Michigan
c/o Area Agency on Aging
29100 Northwestern Highway
Southfield, MI 48034
(313) 262-9218

New Mexico
New Mexico Intergenerational Network
c/o New Mexico Conference of Churches
124 Hermosa SE
Albuquerque, NM 87108
(505) 255-1509

New York
New York State Intergenerational Network
c/o NYC Department of Aging
2 Lafayette Street, 15th floor
New York, NY 10007
(212) 442-1000

Oregon
Oregon Generations Together
PO Box 5181
Eugene, OR 97405
(503) 343-7888

Pennsylvania
Delaware Valley Intergenerational Network
Temple University
1601 North Broad Street, Room 206
Philadelphia, PA 19122

Tennessee
Knoxville Intergenerational Network
1125 College Street
PO Box 9475
Knoxville, TN 37940-9475
(615) 673-8645

Virginia
Let's Link Ages in Virginia
c/o Northern Virginia Community College
3001 North Beauregard Street
Alexandria, VA 22311-5097
(703) 845-6437

Washington
Seattle/King County Generations United
c/o Housing and Human Services
Alaska Building, 6th floor
618 Second Avenue
Seattle, WA 98104
(206) 684-0104

Wisconsin
Wisconsin Intergenerational Network
PO Box 5171
Madison, WI 53705
(608) 238-7936

RESOURCE ORGANIZATIONS: CONTACT INFORMATION
Administration on Aging
Department of Health and Human Services
200 Independence Avenue SW
Washington, DC 20201

National Association of Area Agencies on Aging
1112 16th Street NW
Washington, DC 20036

> Contact them—or your state department on aging—for contact information on your local AAA which can then put you in touch with numerous programs including SCORE and the Senior Community Service Employment Program

National Council on the Aging, Inc.
600 Maryland Avenue SW
Washington, DC 20024

Gray Panthers
311 S. Juniper Street
Philadelphia, PA 19107

Elderhostel
80 Boylston Street #400
Boston, MA 02116

Older Women's League
730 11th Street NW #300
Washington, DC 20001

Green Thumb, Inc.
2000 North 14th Street #800
Arlington, VA 22201

Project Head Start
Department of Health and Human Services
200 Independence Avenue SW
Washington, DC 20201

National Head Start Association
1220 King Street #200
Alexandria, VA 22314

Boy Scouts of America, Inc.
1325 Walnut Hill Lane
Irving, TX 75062

Girl Scouts of America, Inc.
830 Third Avenue
New York, NY 10022

Camp Fire Boys and Girls, Inc.
4601 Madison Avenue
Kansas City, MO 64112-1278

4-H Programs Extension Service
US Department of Agriculture
Washington, DC 20250

Commission on National and Community Service
529 14th Street NW #452
Washington, DC 20045

    Contact to be referred to your state office designated as the "lead agency" for this new federal program

American Association of Retired Persons
1909 K Street NW
Washington, DC 20049

Area Offices:

Area 1—CT, ME, MA, NH, RI, VT
31 St. James Avenue
Boston, MA 02116

Area 2—DE, NJ, NY, PA
225 Market Street #502
Harrisburg, PA 17101

Area 3—DC, KY, MD, NC, VA, WV
1600 Duke Street, 2nd floor
Alexandria, VA 22314

Area 4—AL, FL, GA, MS, SC, TN, Puerto Rico
and the US Virgin Islands
999 Peachtree Street NE #1650
Atlanta, GA 30309

Area 5—IL, IN, MI, OH, WI
2720 Des Plaines Avenue #113
Des Plaines, IL 60018

Area 6—IA, KS, NE, ND, SD, MO, MN
1901 W. 47th Place #104
Westwood, KS 66205

Area 7—AR, LA, NM, OK, TX
8144 Walnut Hill Lane #700 LB-39
Dallas, TX 75321

Area 8—CO, MT, UT, WY
6975 Union Park Center #320
Midvale, UT 84047

Area 9—AZ, CA, HI, NV
4201 Long Beach Blvd. #422
Long Beach, CA 90807

Area 10—AL, ID, OR, WA
9750 Third Avenue NE #400
Seattle, WA 98115

ACTION Agency (including Foster Grandparents and RSVP)
1100 Vermont Avenue NW
Washington, DC 20525

Regional Offices:

Region 1—CT, MA, ME, NH, VT, RI
10 Causeway Street #473
Boston, MA 02222-1039

Region 2—NJ, NY, Puerto Rico, Virgin Islands
6 World Trade Center Building #758
New York, NY 10048-0206

Region 3—KY, MD, DE, OH, PA, VA, WV, DC
U.S. Customs House #108
Second and Chestnut Streets
Philadelphia, PA 19106-2996

Region 4—AL, FL, GA, MS, NC, SC, TN
101 Marietta Street NW #1003
Atlanta, GA 30323-2301

Region 5—IL, IN, IA, MI, MN, WI
175 West Jackson Street #1207
Chicago, IL 60604-2702

Region 6—AR, KS, LA, MO, NM, OK, TX
1100 Commerce Street #6B11
Dallas, TX 75242-0696

(There is no longer a Region 7)

Region 8—CO, WY, MT, NE, ND, SD, UT
Executive Tower Building #2930
1405 Curtis Street
Denver, CO 80202-2349

Region 9—AZ, CA, HI, NV, Guam, American Samoa
211 Main Street #530
San Francisco, CA 94105-1914

Region 10—AL, ID, OR, WA
Jackson Federal Building
915 Second Avenue
Seattle, WA 98174-1103

National Association of RSVP Directors
703 Main Street
Patterson, NJ 07503

National Association of Foster Grandparent Directors
9851 Hamilton Avenue
Detroit, MI 48202

Service Corps of Retired Executives (SCORE)
(an independent program funded by the Small Business
Administration;
409 Third Street SW
Washington, DC 20024
for local office, call your AAA.)

National Association of Retired Federal Employees
1533 New Hampshire Avenue NW
Washington, DC 20036

National Retired Teachers' Association
(a unit of AARP)
1909 K Street NW
Washington, DC 20049

Elverita Lewis Foundation
PO Box 1539
La Quinta, CA 92253

Generations United
c/o Child Welfare League
440 First Street NW #310
Washington, DC 20001

Generations Together
Center for Social and Urban Research
University of Pittsburgh
121 University Place #300
Pittsburgh, PA 15260-5907

Center for Intergenerational Learning
Temple University
1601 North Broad Street
Philadelphia, PA 19122

Lifespan Resources, Inc. (formerly New Age, Inc.)
1212 Roosevelt Street
Ann Arbor, MI 48104

Intergenerational Resource Center
Center for Family Education
Oakton Community College
7701 North Lincoln Avenue
Skokie, IL 60077-2895

Center on Rural Elderly
University of Missouri—Kansas City
5245 Rockhill Road
Kansas City, MO 64110-2499

SELECT BIBLIOGRAPHY

Note: This bibliography lists only materials used in researching this book. For a fuller bibliography of intergenerational articles and books, see Janet Wilson's publication, cited below.

Aging America: Trends and Projections 1991. Washington, DC: US Department of Health and Human Services, 1991.

Allen, Katherine R. "Promoting Family Awareness and Intergenerational Exchange." In *Educational Gerontology,* 13 (1): 43-52, 1987.

Americans Over 55: The Nation's Great Overlooked Resource. NY: Commonwealth Fund, 1991.

Angelis, Jane. *Creating Intergenerational Coalitions: Bottom Up-Top Down Strategies.* Carbondale, IL: Illinois Intergenerational Initiative, 1992.

————. "The Genesis of an Intergenerational Program." In *Educational Gerontology* 18: 317-327, 1992.

————. *Getting Started Now: A Concise Guide to Developing Effective Intergenerational Programs.* Carbondale, IL: Illinois Intergenerational Initiative, 1990.

————. *Intergenerational Service-Learning: Strategies for the Future.* Carbondale, IL: Illinois Intergenerational Initiative, 1990.

Arguelles, Mary. *Before Your Time.* Reading, PA: Generational Resources Exchange, n.d.

Arguelles, Mary and Beata Peck Little. *So Now What?* Reading, PA: Generational Resources Exchange, 1989.

Because You Have so Much to Share: A Guide to Using Older Volunteers. Philadelphia: Big Brothers/Big Sisters, 1990.

Betancourt, Ingrid. "Gente y Cuentos/ People and Stories." In *New Jersey Libraries* 21: 4-9, Winter 1988.

Berkowitz, Lois and Beryl Lieff Benderly. *Building Bridges to Citizenship: How to Create Successful Intergenerational Citizenship Programs.* Alexandria, VA: Close-Up Foundation, 1989.

Bird, Tom. "Five Questions to Test Your Intergenerational Idea." In Kathlyn Thorp. *Intergenerational Programs: A Source for Community Renewal.* Madison, WI: Wisconsin Positive Youth Development Initiative, Inc., 1985.

Bocian, Kathleen and Sally Newman. "Evaluation of Intergenerational Programs: Why and How?" In Sally Newman and Steven W. Brummel, Op. Cit.

Brown, Barbara J. *Programming for Librarians: A How-To-Do-It Manual.* NY: Neal-Schuman Publishers, 1992.

Brummel, Steven W. "Developing an Intergenerational Program." In Sally Newman and Steven W. Brummel, Op. Cit.

Buxton, Kathy. "Intergenerational Library Programs." *California State Library Bulletin*, 28: 21-22, July 1989.

Chase's Annual Events: Special Days, Weeks and Months in 1993. Chicago, IL: Contemporary Books, 1992.

Children Today [special issue on intergenerational programs] 14(5): September-October, 1985.

Close to Home. Towson, MD: ALA Video/Library Video network, 1992. (Video)

Critchell, Mary King and Jacquenette Locker. *Lifecraft: A Guide to Intergenerational Sharing of Activities.* Ann Arbor, MI: Life Span Resources, 1980.

Cuellar, Jose. *Aging and Health: American Indian/Alaskan Native Elders.* Palo Alto, CA: Stanford Geriatric Education Center, 1990.

Directory of Intergenerational Programming. Kansas City, MO: Center on Rural Elderly, 1988.

Dobrez, Cynthia K. "Sharing and Preserving Family Stories." In *Library Journal*, 33(6): 40, February 1987.

Dowd, Frances Smardo. "Latchkey Children: A Community and Public Library Phenomenon." In *Public Library Quarterly*, 10(1): 7-22, 1990.

Dowd, Frances Smardo. *Latchkey Children in the Library and Community.* Phoenix: Oryx Press, 1991.

Dowd, Frances Smardo. "The Public Library and the Latchkey Problem: A Survey." In *School Library Journal*, 35(11): 19-24, July 1989.

Dowst, Brenda S. *Open Waters and Safe Harbors: An Intergenerational Life Skills Curriculum: A Teacher's Guide.* Augusta: Maine Committee on Aging, 1988.

Ensley, Robert F. "Involving Older Adults in Education: The Illinois Intergenerational Initiative." In *Illinois Libraries*, 69 (5): 325-328, May 1987.

Families for Literacy. Sacramento, CA: California State Library, 1992. (15-minute video and guidebook.)

The Family, The Courts, and the Constitution. Washington, DC: National Council on the Aging, Inc., 1985.

Fischer, Denise R. "Families Reading Together: Sharing the Joy." In *Texas Library Journal*, 66 (3): 84-88, Fall 1990.

"Florida Retirees Give Help With Homework and Library Use." In *Library Journal*, 110:22+, September 15, 1985.

The Foster Grandparent Program: A Manual for Planning, Implementing, and Operating the Foster Grandparent Program. La Quinta, CA: Elvirita Lewis Foundation, 1988.

Fowles, Donald G. "Pyramid Power." In *Aging*, 362: 58-59, Winter 1991.

Frazier, Billie H. *Intergenerational Relationships.* Beltsville, MD: National Agricultural Library (Family Information Center), 1990.

Friedman, S. *Closing the Gap: An Intergenerational Discussion Model Guide for Replication.* Kensington, MD: Interages, 1990.

Gordon, S. K. and D.S. Hallauer. "Impact of a Friendly Visiting Program on Attitudes of College Students Toward the Aged." In *Gerontologist*, 16(4): 371-376, 1978.

"Grandparents' Award Links Generations Through Books." In *Library Journal*, 113:20, April 15, 1988.

Green, Marilyn. *Intergenerational Programming in Libraries: A Manual Based on the Experiences of the South Bay Cooperative Library System, 1979-1981.* San Mateo, CA: South Bay Cooperative Library System, 1981.

Gulsvig, Margaret. *First Writes.* Madison, WI: Bi-Folkal Productions, Inc., 1987.

Henkin, Nancy. "Libraries as Catalysts for Linking Generations." Unpublished paper presented at the Library of Congress "Year of the Lifetime Reader" Symposium, 1992.

Henkin, Nancy and Rosalie Minkin. "Full Circle." In *Children Today*, 23-26, September-October, 1985.

Hoopes, James. *Oral History: An Introduction for Students.* Chapel Hill: University of North Carolina Press, 1979.

Intergenerational Activities Program Training Video. Binghamton, NY: Broome County Child Development Council, Inc., 1989. (Video)

Intergenerational Programs: Bringing the Ages Together. Shawnee Mission, KS: RMI Media Productions, 1987. (5 videotapes with guides.)

Irving, Jan. "From Sheep to Shirt: Intergenerational Approaches to Library Programs." In *Illinois Libraries* 67:82-85, January 1985.

Irving, Jan and Robin Currie. *Glad Rags: Stories and Activities Featuring Clothes for Children.* Littleton, CO: Libraries Unlimited, 1987.

Johnson, Sallie. "So You Want To Start Something." In *Kathlyn Thorp.* Op. Cit.

Jones, Clare B. "Grandparents Read to Special Preschoolers." In *Teaching Exceptional Children* p. 36, Fall 1986.

Kandell, Stuart. *Grandparents Tales.* Oakland, CA: Stagebridge, 1988.

Kimmel, Margaret and Elizabeth Segel. *For Reading Out Loud.* rev. ed. NY: Dell, 1988.

Kingson, Eric R. *The Common Stake: The Interdependence of Generations: A Policy Framework for an Aging Society.* Washington, DC: The Gerontological Society of America, 1983.

———. *The Ties That Bind: The Interdependence of Generations.* Cabin John, MD: Seven Locks Press, 1986.

Koftan, Jenelle and Kenneth Koftan. *Long Distance Grandparenting: An Intergenerational Activity Book.* Rose Kill, KS: Spring Creek Publications, 1988.

Lambert, Donna and others. "Planning for Contact Between the Generations: An Effective Approach." In *Gerontologist,* 30 (4): 553-557, August 1990.

Latchkey Children in the Library: Resources for Planners. Chicago: Public Library Association, 1988.

Leonard, Gloria. *Read Aloud Programs: Instructional Manual, Project Summary, and Bibliography.* Seattle, WA: Seattle Public Library, 1987.

Long, Kim. *The Almanac of Anniversaries.* Santa Barbara, CA: ABC-Clio, 1992.

Lubarsky, Nancy. "A Glance at the Past, A Glimpse of the Future." In *Journal of Reading*, 30(6): 520-529, March 1987.

Manheimer, Ronald. *Developing Arts and Humanities Programming with the Elderly*. Chicago: RASD/ American Library Association, 1984.

McDuffie, Winifred G. *Intergenerational Activities Program Handbook*. 3d. ed. Binghamton, NY: Broome County Child Development Council, Inc., 1989.

"Measures of Change." In *US News & World Report*, 107: 66-68, December 25, 1989.

Melcher, Joseph. *Caring is the Key: Building a School-Based Intergenerational Service Program*. Pittsburgh: Generations Together, 1992.

Mersereau, Yvonne and Mary Glover. *A Guide to Community: An Intergenerational Friendship Program Between Young People and Nursing Home Residents*. rev. ed. Madison, WI: Bi-Folkal Productions, Inc., 1992.

Metcalfe, Ruth. "Intergenerational Library Service: Implications for Ohio's Public Libraries." In *State Library of Ohio News*, 49(7):2, April 1992.

Moldeven, Meyer. *A Grandpa's Notebook: Ideas and Stories to Encourage Grandparent-Grandchild Interaction, Communication, and Well-Being*. 2d. ed. Del Mar, CA: the author, 1992. (Contact: PO Box 71, Del Mar, CA 92014-0071.)

Monsour, Margaret and Carole Talan. *Library-Based Family Literacy Projects*. Chicago: ALA, 1993.

Multiethnic Calendar. Berkeley, CA: Berkeley Public Library, 1992.

Murphy, Mary Brugger. *A Guide to Intergenerational Programs*. Washington, DC: National Association of State Units on Aging, 1984.

"New Views on Life Spans Alter Forecasts on Elderly." In *New York Times*, p. A1, November 16, 1992.

Newman, Sally and Steven W. Brummel. *Intergenerational Programs: Imperatives, Strategies, Impacts, Trends*. NY: Haworth Press, 1989.

Nickse, Ruth S. *Family Literacy in Action: A Survey of Successful Programs*. Syracuse, NY: New Readers Press, 1990.

————. *The Noises of Literacy: An Overview of Intergenerational and Family Literacy Programs*. Washington, DC: OERI, 1989 and *Family and*

Intergenerational Literacy Programs: An Update of Noises of Literacy. Washington, DC: OERI, 1990.

Nowicke, Terry and Laquitta Denton. "Give Us Books, Give Us Wings: Seniors Sharing Books With Children." In *Colorado Libraries*, 15:13, December 1989.

"Oklahoma Programs Focus on 'Dirty Thirties'." In *Insight*, Fall 1984.

Older Volunteers: A Valuable Resource. Washington, DC: American Association of Retired Persons, 1986.

Orientation for Youth: Aging and Nursing Homes. Madison, WI: Bi-Folkal Productions, Inc., 1992. (Video.)

Pearson, L.R. "NCLIS/RSVP Pilot Project to Aid Latchkey Children." In *American Libraries*, 19:745-46, October 1988.

Perspectives on Aging. [special issue on intergenerational programs], 15(6): 1-32, November/December 1986.

"Portrait of a Nation in Numbers: Findings of the US Census." In *Facts on File*, 52: 468-473, June 25, 1992.

Prete, Barbara. "Family Literacy: An Intergenerational Approach." In *Publishers Weekly*, 237:38, May 25, 1990.

A Profile of Older Americans 1992. Washington, DC: American Association of Retired Persons, 1992.

"Prospects for Elderly Vary Widely By Sex, Census Says." In *New York Times*, p. A1, November 10, 1992.

Quezada, Shelley and Ruth Nickse. *Community Collaborations for Family Literacy.* NY: Neal-Schuman Publishers, 1993.

Richardson, Julee. *Aging and Health: Black American Elders.* Palo Alto, CA: Stanford Geriatric Education Center, 1990.

Rizzo, Gaye. "Grandma Comes to a Branch Library: A Foster Grandparent Makes Her Mark." In *American Libraries*, 22(9): 904, October 1991.

Robotham, John S. and Lydia LaFleur. *Library Programs: How to Select, Plan, and Produce Them.* Metuchen, NJ: Scarecrow Press, 1976.

Rosen, Nancy. *The HISTOP Manual.* Lansing, MI: Michigan Council for the Humanities, 1983.

"The RSVP Intergenerational Library Assistance Project." In *Journal of Youth Services in Libraries*, 2:10, Fall 1988.

Rubery, Nancy M. "A Grand Idea: The Grandreading Project." In *School Library Journal*, 36(1):42, January 1990.

Rubin, Rhea Joyce. *Of a Certain Age: A Guide to Contemporary Fiction Featuring Older Adults*. Denver: ABC-CLIO, 1990.

Rubin, Rhea Joyce and Gail McGovern. *Working With Older Adults: A Handbook for Libraries*. 3d. ed. Sacramento, CA: California State Library Foundation, 1990.

Scannell, Tess and Angela Roberts. *State and Local Intergenenerational Coalitions and Networks: A Compendium of Profiles*. Washington, DC: Generations United, 1992.

Sheppard, Judy. *Silver Threads Handbook*. Oak Grove, OR: Clackamas County Area Agency on Aging, 1985.

Shuldiner, David. *Humanities for Older Adults: A Brief Guide for Developing Programs and Resources*. Hartford: Connecticut State Department on Aging, 1991.

Slaybaugh, Charles. *The Grandparents' Catalog*. NY: Doubleday, 1986.

Stage for Memory. Brooklyn, NY: Elders Share the Arts, 1992.

The State of America's Children 1991. Washington, DC: Children's Defense Fund, 1991.

The States Speak: A Report on Intergenerational Initiatives. Ann Arbor, MI: New Age, Inc., 1985.

Strategies for Linking the Generations: Report of the 1981 White House Conference on Aging Mini-Conference on Intergenerational Cooperation and Exchange. Washington, DC: National Council on the Aging, Inc., 1981.

Strickland, Charlene. "Intergenerational Reading: Encouraging the Grandlap." In *Wilson Library Bulletin*, 65(4): 46-48+, December 1990.

Struntz, Karen A. and Shari Reville. *Growing Together: An Intergenerational Sourcebook*. La Quinta, CA: Elverita Lewis Foundation, 1985.

Struntz, Karen A. and Shari Reville. *United States Intergenerational Activities Directory 1985: An Addendum to Growing Together*. La Quinta, CA: Elverita Lewis Foundation, 1985.

Talan, Carole, producer. *Families for Literacy*. Sacramento, CA: California State Library, 1992. (Video and guide.)

Thorp, Kathlyn. *Intergenerational Programs: A Resource for Community Renewal*. Madison, WI: Wisconsin Positive Youth Development Initiative, Inc., 1985.

Tice, Carol. *Developing a Curriculum of Caring: Intergenerational Programs in Schools*. Ann Arbor, MI: Teaching-Learning Communities, 1983.

Tice, Carol. *Linking the Generations: Intergenerational Programs: A Wingspread Report*. Racine, WI: Johnson Foundation, Inc., 1982.

A Time and Place for Sharing: A Practical Guide for Developing Intergenerational Programs. South Pasadena, CA: The Beverly Foundation, 1984.

Together is Better. . .Let's Read: ALA National Reading Program Guide. Chicago: ALA, 1992.

Turetzky, Shelly and Marlene Lee. "Prime Time: An Intergenerational Literacy Program." In *Florida Libraries*, 35(6): 121-122, Auggust/September 1992.

"US Elderly Are Growing Steadily More Multicultural." In *Wall Street Journal*, p. B1, February 3, 1993.

Ventura-Merkel, Catherine and Lorraine Lidoff. *Community Planning for Intergenerational Programming*. Washington, DC: NCOA, 1983.

Ventura-Merkel, Catherine. *Strategies for Change: Building State and Local Coalitions on Intergenerational Issues and Programs*. Washington, DC: Generations United, 1990.

Ventura-Merkel, Catherine and Elaine Parks. *Intergenerational Programs: A Catalogue of Profiles*. Washington, DC: National Council on the Aging, Inc., 1984.

"Volunteers in Public Libraries: Issues and Viewpoints." In *Public Library Quarterly*, 5: 29-40, Winter 1984.

Wade, Maureen and Susan Patron. *Grandparents and Books: Trainer's Manual*. rev. ed. Sacramento: California State Library, 1991.

Wigginton, Eliot. *Foxfire* series. New York: Doubleday, 1975-1989.

Wilder, Roslyn. *Step Into My Life*. Upper Montclair, NJ: Encomium Arts, Inc., 1993.

Wilms, Denise. "Contemporary Issues: Intergenerational Relationships." In *Booklist*, 82:1318-1320, May 1, 1986.

Wilson, Janet O. *Intergenerational Books Are Timely: Selected, Annotated Bibliography of Titles for Children and Youth, Preschool Through Grade Twelve*. Pittsburgh: Generations Together, 1992.

————. *Intergenerational Readings 1980-1992: A Bibliography of Books, Journal Articles, Manuals, Papers, Curricula, Bibliographies, Directories, Newsletters, Data Bases, and Videos*. Pittsburgh: Generations Together, 1992.

————. ed. *Intergenerational Stories for Children and Youth: A Selected, Annotated Bibliography 1980-1988*. Pittsburgh: Generations Together, 1989.

Wood, Joan. *Bringing Generations Together: A Listing of Intergenerational Programming Sources*. Pekin, IL: Pekin Public Library, 1992.

————. *Life Spectrum Programming: A Community Model Plan*. Pekin, IL: Pekin Public Library, 1992.

Ziemba, Judes and others. "A Magic Mix: After School Programs in a Nursing Home." In *Children Today*, pp. 9-13, November-December 1988.

Zimmerman, William. *How to Tape Instant Oral Biographies*. rev. ed. NY: Bantam, 1990.

INDEX